To

D. Dave

+ Janet

Cogdall

D1367262

True Gold

History and
Adventure in
Sacramento
and the
Gold Country

From Indians To Arnold
- Map To The Gold
- Adventure Tour

Greg Velm

The Sutter Buttes, a stand-alone mini mountain range near Colusa.
Great Wall by Hugh Gorman.

TRUE GOLD

History and Adventure
in
Sacramento and the Gold Country

From Indians to Arnold

by

Greg Velm

Copyright© 2006 by Greg Velm

Library of Congress Control Number: 2005909584

ISBN: 0-9774819-0-5
[New Format ISBN: 9780977481903]

truegold.org

Cabin in the Sky
SAN: 257-6244
3524 Dutch Way
Carmichael, CA 95608
USA

Printed in China

To Jeanette Smith Voelm,
my wife, who helped me
discover true gold.

Peaceful nature in the middle of the home of 2,000,000 people, the American River that began the Gold Rush flows toward downtown Sacramento. The Bike Trail on the left goes through 33 miles of nature from the spot the gold miners landed in Old Sacramento to Folsom Lake.
Photo: Randy Smith

TRUE GOLD

History and Adventure
In Sacramento and the Gold Country

- FORWARD -

Between the mountains and the ocean, where rivers come together and flow on to the sea, Sacramento and the Gold Country was one of the richest natural areas on earth even before the discovery of gold. It still is.

Early explorers talked about a beautiful country, riding all day under the shade of oak trees, surrounded by deer and antelope. Indians lived here for thousands of years, mostly in peace, never having to move far to find food or a swimming hole.

Sometimes from a hill top, people could see families of grizzly bears browsing along in different directions.
All this changed with the rush for gold in 1849. But even today in what is now the 22nd largest metropolitan area in the United States, rivers and mountains still bring the peace of nature to the capital of California. As the center of the largest Gold Rush in the history of the world, Sacramento is full of excitement - past and present. The rush is not over. History is not just the past: it is how we got here and therefore who we are, with some clues to who we might become.
The history of True Gold is our real story.

A note on money: quoting earning and prices in 1800's dollars confuses readers used to current values. Gold was sold for $20 an ounce in the 1800's; it was $400 an ounce in 2005. That's not a change in the value of gold; it is a change in the value of money—a change that had been going on throughout history. The Consumer Price Index, the dollar cost of living, has increased by more than 20 times since the Gold Rush. In this book, prices are sometimes shown the way they were originally reported in 1800's money and always in the amount they would be worth in modern dollars-- using a multiple of 20 to take into account both gold and CPI changes.

Valuable editorial assistance came from, Bob Greeley,
Steve Beck, Bob LaPerriere, Anne Ofsink and Georgia Jones.

James Henley of the Sacramento Archives
is a guiding light for all area history.

Artistic credit goes to Eric Warp, Noel Neuburger,
Meyers Photography, Dave Sherwood,
Catherine Oshiro, Windy Kahana, Judi Decker and Bud Plant.

Thanks to Clare Ellis of the Sacramento Library History Room,
Gary Kurutz of the California State Library, Jill Stockinger of
Carmichael Library, and the volunteers of
the Folsom History Museum.

Any mistakes are mine and I look forward to the kind of
improvements of future writers who will join me and my predecessors
in the periodic revision that is history.

Greg Velm, 2006

Chapter One
INTRODUCTION
∽

Having accomplished my purpose of landing Captain Sutter at the junction of the American and Sacramento rivers with his men and his freight, the following morning we left him there, and headed the two vessels for Yerba Buena.
As we moved away, Captain Sutter gave us a parting salute of nine guns—the first ever fired at that place—which produced a most remarkable effect. As the heavy report of the guns and the echoes died away, the camp of the little party was surrounded by hundreds of Indians, who were excited and astonished at the unusual sound.

A large number of deer, elk, and other animals on the plains were startled, running to and fro, stopping to listen, their heads raised, full of curiosity and wonder, seemingly attracted and fascinated to the spot, while from the interior of the adjacent wood the howls of wolves and coyote filled the air, and immense flocks of water fowl flew wildly about over the camp.

John Sutter, searching for high ground and a safe landing place, chose a spot on the south bank of the American River, just above where it comes together with the wider Sacramento, to build a fort that he dreamed would be the beginning of a great empire. The next building to the east was 1,000 miles away.

Snow geese. Even in a settled land, some of the "immense flocks of water fowl" William Heath Davis saw in 1839 are still here. **Photo: Tom Myers**

Sacramento with riverboats.
Photo: Tom Meyers

He picked this place so he could grow wheat and hay in the fertile central valley, hunt deer, beaver and elk at the base of the snow capped Sierra and take a boat down the river to San Francisco Bay. He wanted to be free and make money.

He thought the rivers would lead people up to the mountains to find trees for building houses and metal for making tools. The rivers could also lead people down from the mountains in wagon trains to Sutter's Fort and provide water power for the lumber and flour mills he hoped to build. Sutter wanted to be lord of a farming kingdom; he never dreamed the rivers would lead to gold.

Sutter's peaceful dream was overrun by the Gold Rush. He didn't get everything he wanted, but he got enough for a comfortable life. Sutter's dream set the stage for the dreams of a million other people. His ranch fields, even though he did not own them any more, grew into a vast food growing empire. The dirt trail no wider than your shoulders grew to be freeways, railroads, ships and planes that made his settlement the capital of the richest state in the most powerful nation in the world.

A muddy landing he used for supplies on the Sacramento River grew into the city of Sacramento to support the miners who came for the Gold Rush that started in the foothills at Sutter's mill. His ranch became one of the largest metropolitan areas in the United States as jobs grew from gold to crops, government and high tech.

Already a transportation center with hundreds of stage coaches wheeling through the dusty streets every day, Sacramento in 1869, became the western end of the first railroad across America. During 1860 to 1861, the Pony Express galloped through the foothills to Sacramento. The land where Indians and wild animals roamed changed in one adventurous lifetime to a place famous around the world.

During the early years, gold and growing food were the major ways to make money. Mining changed from small groups of men looking for gold in stream beds to hard rock mines that tunneled underground for miles. Some miners used huge water nozzles to blast gold bearing hills

A miner's dreams. **From: PI**

and others dredged with floating machines the size of a house that scooped up gravel and picked out the gold. As exciting as gold was, even more money lay in the fields and sunshine which brought thousands of hopeful new farmers. Some grew crops that never quite made it, like the orange dream that founded suburban Citrus Heights and Orangevale. Most farmers raised food that still grows today like apples, grapes and almonds.

The rivers carried gold from quartz veins deep within the earth, and their gravel glistened with flakes and nuggets that touched off the California Gold Rush, the greatest gold discovery and the largest peaceful mass migration in all world history. In some ways, it is still going on.

But rivers don't always do what people want. The Nisenan Indians, over hundreds of years, learned to live with the rivers and mountains. They caught salmon, gathered acorns and dug up wild onions to go with the roasted meat of elk, deer and antelope.

As the rivers dwindled to a warm stream in the hot valley summer, the Nisenan gathered food on the cooler slopes of the Sierra. Most of the time they lived together peacefully with each other and the dangerous grizzly bears that hunted near them. In wet winters, they moved to high ground to escape the floods they knew were coming. The Native Americans warned the settlers repeatedly when floods were approaching. Again and again the settlers ignored the Indians and ended up swimming away from their flooded houses.

Too many people think they can conquer nature rather than live with it, and that bad idea has caused a lot of trouble. As flood after flood washed through Sacramento in the 1800's, Chinese and Hawaiian laborers carried thousands of baskets of soil up on the levees to build a wall around the city. At the same time, hydraulic miners in the foothills blasting water to uncover gold, dumped thousands of tons of soil into the river that raised flood waters faster then the workers could build levees.

As floods continued, the city took more drastic action. The river itself was moved and straightened. Wagon loads of soil and rocks were dumped in the

14

streets 8 or 10 feet deep to raise the streets above flood level. All downtown Sacramento streets near the river were raised a story, leaving old front doors in the basement. Finally, in the world's first environmental court decision, destructive hydraulic mining was banned.

Even with the addition of dams in the 1950's, the rivers that meet at Sacramento still go on a rampage every ten years or so, most recently in 1986 and 1997. The U.S. Army Corps of Engineers and the U.S. Bureau of Reclamation helped by a host of other state and local water agencies—manage the rivers with dams and diversions trying to protect the salmon and other fish that once thronged in the river while serving an increasing population of human beings.

There is no way to stop a river; dams only slow it down. Nature is like a tiger in a show, contained for now but really never tame. Thoughtful management does work: in the old days more than 100,000 adult Chinook salmon swam up the American River every year. Dams cut their spawning area and the fish run

shrank to a few thousand. Now with timed water releases and hatchery help, the salmon are coming back. The American, Sacramento, Yuba and Cosumnes Rivers are remarkably clean, even as they flow through the middle of one of the largest metro areas in the United States. Along the American runs one of the longest urban bike trails in the world- only occasionally can riders see a building as they pedal without crossing traffic for 33 miles all the way from the spot where the first 49er stepped ashore in Old

It was easy to spear fish during salmon runs. There were so many fish it seemed to the people that they could almost walk across the river on their backs.
From: SAMCC

15

Sacramento almost to within sight of the first big gold strike at Mormon Island. But river protection is only as good as the alert citizen groups who guard against private interests and unwise development.

Sacramento and the Gold Country are history that is still alive, handed on from the Indians to Jed Smith and his fur trappers under attack; from explorers Fremont and Kit Carson to settlers James Marshall and Sutter surprised by gold; from the early miners who swarming over the rivers to those who used gold to build a new life, from the Chinese who ground-sluiced those mysterious mines near Folsom to people who struggled to build businesses; from the hopeful farmers working to grow olives and oranges, to modern agriculture trying to make money and feed people while doing what is necessary to sustain the environment.

Maybe we will learn from the mistakes of the past and build on the best dreams of our ancestors.

Maybe not, but we could. Like the rivers that slowly roll glistening rocks though ancient canyons even as you read this, change is inevitable, **but true gold is there to be found.**

16

Chapter Two
NATIVE AMERICANS
Lively, lively, we are lots of people.
Dance Song, Maidu

BEFORE HISTORY

Prehistoric Indians in the Sacramento area lived for thousands of years in a wet paradise, challenging but wonderful. If the time native people have lived here were a deep swimming pool, written history after the settlers would cover only the top two inches. For thousands of years before settlers arrived to write history, the Sacramento Valley was a winter and spring wetland, allowing food to grow almost everywhere. Indians recognized hundreds of plants that are still here today; in the spring flowers were everywhere. Indians ate ground acorns, sort of like mashed potatoes, plus more different kinds of berries, fruit, fish and meat than we have today.

The forest was always close; people were surrounded by elk, antelope, bears, deer, wildcats and mountain lions. The river banks were home to more beavers and river otters than are still around today. Water birds included so many ducks, geese, cranes, herons, and swans that a stream to the north was named Feather River. In the foothills, there were quail, woodpeckers, hawks, owls, eagles, and even condors with a wing span wider than a car. At least 25 species of fish lived in the American River including salmon (delicious and almost filling the river when they spawned), trout, suckers, perch, and sturgeon sometimes weighing more than 500 pounds.

First People

Most likely, the first people who lived in California came from Siberia across the frozen Bering Straits down through Alaska. Expanding out, small groups from Oregon and Nevada pushed over the mountains into what turned out to be a beautiful new home in California.

California has been lived in for at least 12,000 years, not much more than one tenth of the time that human beings have been spreading out over the earth.

The first people lived near enough to the river to catch fish but on high ground so that they could escape flood waters. They built their houses near Valley Oak groves because they loved the acorn food from these trees. Native Americans are called Indians because Christopher Columbus thought he had gotten to India when he reached the new world and, as wrong as he was, no one ever changed the name.

Archeologists know where some of the native villages were because they have found stone tools and bones. Rivers change with time, so villages were built in new areas, always near water and oak trees. Indians moved when they needed to; they could build a fresh house out of branches and leaves in a few hours.

Early Horizon
(2500 B.C. - 1000 B.C.)

The first people lived near the American River in the years from 2500 B.C. to 1000 B.C, about the same time as the ancient Greeks half the world away. The Early Horizon people used heavy spears to hunt big animals like deer, antelope, and elk - there were herds of them near the rivers. It is still possible to find the spear heads of Early Horizon hunters: look for heavy points, usually made from black stone different from the rocks around them. Indians worked for weeks to make spear points with nothing but other rocks for tools.

Early Indians also ate plants and seeds. They ground this food on a metate, a flat piece of stone, with a smaller stone called mano. Such cooking tools are still used today by some Indians in Mexico.

The early people buried their dead in well-organized cemeteries. A body was placed in the ground fully stretched out with its head pointed to the setting sun in the west. Most of the graves contained artifacts, valuable personal property like necklaces and tools. Usually when artifacts are found in graves, it is because people thought their dead friends would need them in a later life.

Natives from this period can be distinguished from the later Middle and Late Horizons by the kind of shell beads they wore and the way they were buried. Made primarily from shells found in the Pacific Ocean, the beads came from trading with Indians from

There are still hollowed out rocks used by Indians for grinding acorn food scattered around the countryside. **From: CSL**

the coast. With carbon dating and by studying many different burial grounds, archeologists learned how what was popular in a shell necklace changed over thousands of years. Like pottery dishes in other parts of the world, Indian beads give us an idea of the dates of villages founded years before anyone wrote down history.

Early Horizon village locations have been found on just on the Sacramento River, not in other places. But more and more people came to live here, so from the next Middle Horizon period there are remains of villages along all the rivers.

Middle Horizon
(1000 B.C. - A.D. 300)

All periods in history are just names to describe trends in the way people lived; like all trends they overlap each other. The Middle Horizon is the same time that the world was writing down the great religious books like the

Bible. The Indians had religions too, but they didn't write; they sang and danced their beliefs.

A major trend that sets apart the people of the Middle Horizon is the way they got food. Previously, hunters speared big land animals like deer and elk, now they did more fishing.
By catching lots of salmon and other fish, hunters made food for more people to live along the river. When scientists look at skeletons from this period they can tell that people were healthy because fewer babies died and adults lived longer.

Spears were smaller during the Middle Horizon because Indians hunted smaller animals. Plant foods were ground up with a mortar and pestle, more like a bowl and grinder, instead of the almost flat mano and metate used in the Early Horizon. You can still find Indian grinding bowls built into big rocks in pretty places along the river, overlooking hillside meadows and near mountain passes.

B urying the dead also changed in this period. Bodies had their knees drawn up to their chests and were placed in the ground on their back or side. Their heads were not pointed in any special direction and less than half had valuables with them. A new type of abalone shell necklace was popular during this period. That is how we can identify the trend to Middle Horizon.

L ate Horizon
(A.D. 300 - 1769)

The Late Horizon period started with the introduction of the bow and arrow near A.D. 300 and ended with the Spanish Missions in 1769.

In the Late Horizon, more bodies were cremated after they died. Sharp stone points that can still be found were smaller and lighter, designed for use on arrows more than spears. New kinds of shell beads were in fashion. By the end of the Late Horizon, a few European items like glass beads and knives were being traded to the Indians of the Sacramento area by neighboring Indian populations, before any of the Indians had ever met a settler.

Finding Indian Sites

Hundreds of archaeological sites have been recorded on the banks

Indians had their life on the line with nature. **From: Colliers, 23**

of the rivers and in the foothills of the Sacramento area. These sites range from large villages to grinding holes in the natural bedrock. The majority of these places are from the later years. Archeologists do not publicize these places because they do not want souvenir hunters to mess them up; these sites contain the only clues we have about the people who came before us.

If you find tools, grinding rocks or bones, report them to an archeologist. You might learn something about your find or even contribute to history.

Indians Around Sacramento and the Foothills

The Nisenan were the south-ernmost of three groups known as the Maidu. Like many tribes, the name Nisenan is the mem-ber's way of saying "the people". They didn't know much about other tribes and would have had trouble understanding even a northern Maidu. The Nisenan were a social people who liked to make friends, but they did not travel far from their homes.

The Nisenan lived on the eastern side of the Sacramento River from the valley to about half way up the Sierra Nevada. Their territory extended from the Bear and Yuba Rivers in the north to the Cosumnes River in the south, from what is now Marysville to Lodi. Although they may have gone hunting or fishing in the Sierra during the summer, there are no signs of permanent villages above the 3000 foot elevation. Within the Nisenan population, valley and foothill people were different. The valley Indians lived in larger villages and ate more fish; the mountain Nisenan lived in small groups and ate more animals. The two groups may have even fought sometimes.

Early explorers 200 years ago reported many Nisenan villages along the rivers. As late as two years before the Gold Rush, there were more than 20,000 Indians and only 500 settlers in the area. Indian houses looked like big dome tents, but instead of cloth they were covered with leaves or soil. Most California Indian villages had just a few families because there were only enough fish, animals and acorns nearby to feed 50 or 100 people. They were not farmers—although they might clear some ground, they depended on food that grew by itself. A few villages contained 500 or more Indians. Even though it took hard work to find food for all these people, they enjoyed living together.

The larger villages always had dance houses, as much as 50 feet across and partly underground for parties, meetings and ceremonies. They had sweat houses like a smoky sauna made of branches; when the Indians got hot they homes. There were big acorn storage baskets on stilts; the Indians just opened the bottom and dropped out as many acorns as they needed. Most of the time they had plenty to eat. Indians liked to have some open country around their village so they could watch for possibly threatening animals or strangers.

THE ATTACK.

Usually it was the Indians who were being attacked and, either way, arrows were no match for guns. From: CSL

would run outside and jump in the cold stream. To make sure they stayed warm during the day, Indians always picked sunny, southwestern clearings for their

Elsewhere in the old days in many parts of the world, women and girls usually had to do lots of the work but never got to be leaders. The Nisenan were not like that - women could be shamans, a combination of priest and doctor, the most important person in the village. The men did most of the hunting and fighting as well as leading ceremonies in the dance and sweat house, but they listened to what the women said. There were not countries or states in Nisenan times, just villages with local leaders. Each village had a town crier to call out the news and remind people about gatherings. The whole village cried when someone died. People burned objects they loved with their dead friends, either as a tribute or to help them in an imagined time when they would live again.

The Nisenan were hunters, gatherers, and fishermen. During the cold months, all the village stayed close around their fires. When it got warmer they spread out looking for food. Indians were good at creeping up on animals or setting traps. They gathered the seeds and berries they liked most when they were ripe. They trapped or speared fish when they swam up the streams. Sometimes they captured deer by setting the dry grass on fire all around them.

Since it was warm most of the year, the Nisenan did not need much clothing. Women often wore nothing but a short apron made from bark or leaves. Woven into two pieces, the women tucked the apron between their legs when they sat down. Men were often naked, but when it got cold everybody put on deer or rabbit skin blankets to keep warm. Most of the time, the Nisenan were barefoot -their feet got used to walking over dirt, sticks and rocks. Moccasins, made from a single piece of leather tied together above the ankle were used, with leggings, for long journeys or hunting expeditions. Pictures of Indians often show them with more clothes on than they usually wore - this is either to keep from shocking people or because the Indians in the picture had borrowed some of the settlers way of dressing.

Indians made bows from wood that would bend without breaking. The string was a long tendon, part of a deer muscle. Arrows were made from hardwood and usually had three feathers tied to the shaft. Arrow heads were carefully sharpened for hours from obsidian or hardwood such as oak--sometimes they were made to spread on contact so that the arrows would be difficult to get out. Spears, used only in war by the later Indians, were made from willow and also had obsidian points. Obsidian is a shiny, hard, black volcanic glass from the mountains and can be made very sharp.

Mission Period 1769 - 1839

For thousands of years, the Indians had California to themselves. Then about the time of the American Revolution, the Spanish started building missions along the coast 100 miles from the Nisenan.

In 1806 the Spanish soldier Gabriel Moraga traveling north along the Sacramento River "found multitudes of Indians everywhere along the streams." When he came back two years later the Indians tried to drive him away. This was difficult because Moraga had guns that frightened them and armor that could stop the Indian's arrows.

Jedediah Smith, an American fur trapper exploring with his men, camped on the American near where it meets the Sacramento River in 1828. When the Spanish heard that Smith and

other trappers were near, they named the stream he was on El Rio de los Americanos: the American River, probably hoping the Americans would stay there and not cause trouble for the Spanish.

Jedediah was a gentle man and tried to make friends by giving presents to the Indians. But when some Indians surrounded him and, thinking his guns were just big sticks, got ready to attack, Smith felt he had no choice but to shoot some of them. He saw "Indians by hundreds but wilder than antelopes running and screaming in every direction." Jedediah thought the American River should be named the Wild River because the I Indians were so wild.

The Spanish never settled inland, so the Nisenan had a few more years of peace. But while the settlers did not come at once, passing trappers spread diseases. Epidemics of malaria, measles, smallpox and other diseases to which the Indians had no resistance wiped out more than half of the California Indians in the 1830's before they had ever seen a settler. Children and old people died first, but eventually whole villages were sick so there was no

PROTECTING THE SETTLERS.

Indians were massacred at the slightest excuse. Almost wiped out by disease and by settlers who were themselves frightened immigrants, the Indian spirit survived.

From CSL.

one to bury the dead. People kept dying and before the Gold Rush even started, less that one in three of the once proud Nisenan were still alive. Whole villages disappeared forever and the Indians that were left were sad and weak from losing most of their family.

Sutter Period
1839 - 1850

With many of the Indians gone, there was room for new settlers. The first settlers were not Mexican or American but, amazingly enough, a man from Switzerland named John Sutter with 10 helpers from Hawaii. Sutter had left his wife and children back in Switzerland. Trying to find a way to make money to pay off the debts he still owed back home, Sutter traveled from city to city in the United States and then on to Hawaii. With his Hawaiian helpers, he sailed to Monterey and talked the Mexican government into giving him most of the land around what is now Sacramento. When Sutter and his workers built Sutter's Fort years before the Gold Rush, it was the only large building in a hundred miles of wilderness. It still stands today in downtown Sacramento.

The Indian population was too weak to fight Sutter. When they stole cattle, he attacked them with guns and cannon. Many Nisenan had to work for Sutter just to get help for their families. He gave them some food and clothing, but many continued to die. While Sutter did not treat Indians as equals, he was one of the only settlers to pay them for their work.

Sutter had more than 300 Indian employees working for him harvesting wheat before the Gold Rush, but they could look around them and see deserted Nisenan villages along every stream. When the Gold Rush started, the few free Indians who survived were hiding in the hills.

American Period
1850 - 1900

Unfortunately for the Indians, their hills were full of gold. Only a few days after the United States officially took over California, gold was discovered in the beautiful valley the Indians called Coloma, the heart of Nisenan country. Of course the Indians had known about the glistening rocks all along, but they did not think rocks were worth fighting over. *"The spirit that owns the yellow metal is a bad spirit"*, a Nisenan chief is said to have warned. *"It will drive you crazy if you possess it."*

In the beginning, the precious gold was good news for some Indians. In the first year before they were overrun by gold crazy '49ers, most of the early miners were Indians. They panned with baskets, blankets, anything they had. They found gold but were often cheated out of their profit or forced to work as slaves for miners.

While a few people tried to help the Indians, most of the thousands of gold hungry Americans who rushed into California just wanted the Indians out of the way, dead or alive. At a time when slavery was still legal in the southern states and many Americans thought of Indians as sub-human dangerous pests, the government actually paid bounty hunters to kill peaceful Indian men, women and children. Young Indians were taken from their parents and sold as indentured servants.

When starving Indians stole food or fought back against rape or beatings, they were often killed along with any other Indians unlucky enough to be in the area. For the next 10 years Indian villages were burned and the people hunted like animals.

By 1860 there were so few Nisenan they were almost forgotten by the settlers. Only ten years after the Gold Rush, of the original 300,000 Indians who lived in all of California before the Europeans came, only 1 out of 20 survived.

Most Americans today are a mixture of many cultures. More and more people are proud of whatever Indian heritage they may have; the number of people who say they have Indian blood in California is now approaching the number of Indians who lived here at the time the Spanish started the first mission. Indians were the real pioneers - they lived in relative peace for 10 times as long as the Americans have been in California. And they knew a harmony with nature modern society is still trying to find.

Some Village Locations

1.Pujune.
Pujune was the main meeting place for Nisenan who lived along the Sacramento River for a few

miles both north and south of the mouth of the American River. It was where the American and the Sacramento rivers come together.

2. Sekumne.

As Pujune controlled the mouth of the American River and part of the Sacramento, Sekumne was an important village upward the Sierra foothills on the American. It was on the north bank of the River, toward downtown from Cal Expo.

3. Kadema.

Kadema was a major village on the south side of the river near Watt Avenue Bridge.

Kadema is one of two villages of Valley Nisenan on the American River known to have a dance house. There were big celebrations at Kadema.

There were at least ten other villages around the Sacramento area when the Gold Rush began. You can catch a faint echo of the natural richness of Nisenan life before the settlers came by visiting the California State Indian Museum, the Effie Yeaw Nature Center, or by standing alone where an ancient oak tree overlooks the river.

*Indian village with its large meeting house near the river. This could have been any time for thousands of years before the coming of the settlers. Detail from the Great Wall of Carmichael **by Hugh Gorman.***

Chapter Three
HISPANIC CALIFORNIA

**A great country, the most peaceful and quiet in the world.
One lives better than in the most cultured courts of Europe.**
*Spanish California Governor
Diego de Borica, 1794*

Spain claimed California a few years before the American Revolution by building missions and small forts. Mexico gained its independence from Spain 50 years later and got to run California for 25 years until they lost it to the United States.

There were no Spanish missions near Sacramento; early settlement in California was close to the Pacific Ocean. Hispanic officials liked to live within thirty miles of the coast were they could have ships nearby for supplies and a way to escape if there was an Indian uprising. The Spanish wanted to convert the Indians to their Roman Catholic religion and teach them to be farmers.

The way it looked to the explorers. **Photo: Tom Meyers**

With Indian labor, they built 21 missions on a trail that stretched from San Francisco to Mexico. Also with the help of the Indians, they raised cattle on the wide open California hills. There were never more than 7,000 Hispanic people in California but they got thousands of Indians to work for them.

San Francisco was founded in 1776, the same year that across the continent, America was declaring its independence from Britain. A few years before, Pedro Fages led the first small European exploration around the San Francisco Bay, He reported "a round bay like a great Lake large enough for all the armadas of Spain." Early explorers stared in wonder at spouting whales in the Bay and thousands of elk swimming across the channel. Fages was given a kindly welcome a few miles east of San Pablo Bay by "bearded and light-complexioned" Indians.

The Spanish wanted to go around the north side of the Bay to the Point Reyes peninsula they had seen from their sailing ships. But their expedition was on horseback and they couldn't get across the Carquinez Strait.

Looking along the shores of the Strait, Fages' men saw at least five large Indian villages. The Indians were so curious and unafraid that they paddled a mile across the strait that the Spanish couldn't cross to get a closer look at them. Fages climbed a hill and got a view of an unknown delta land of channels and islands leading toward what would one day be Sacramento. That's as close as Europeans got in the 1700's. The first edition of the Encyclopedia Britannica published around the time of the American Revolution said it was not known if California was a peninsula or an island. It turned out to be neither.

The Spanish sometimes chased Indians who had run away from the missions or taken stolen cattle into the Central Valley. While the Spanish never settled inland, Hispanic occupation devastated Indians along the coast. There were an estimated 72,000 coastal Indians at the beginning of the Spanish period; through disease and violence only 18,000 were left 75 years later at the end of Hispanic rule.

In the early 1800's, Spanish Californians finally managed to get to what would become

Into the wild. - *From SAMCC*

Sacramento. Gabriel Moraga named the big river Sacramento and the river later named the town. Moraga was probably thinking of the services of his own Roman Catholic church, but sacramento comes from the word "sacred" that was already old when his religion was born. Sacred means something that connects people to God.

American Explorers

Moraga had been gone about 20 years when Jedediah Smith and his men explored the Sacramento and American rivers in 1827. Jedediah was on a 3,000 mile search for beaver because they had been trapped until there were none left in the eastern and central United States. Hats worn by fashionable men in the big cities of American and Europe were made from the fur of these river animals. Just one skin was worth the equivalent of more than $300 in modern dollars in London and there were thousands of beaver in the northern California streams.

Jedediah's party had a wild time. Once he was helped across a river by Indians who acted friendly until they got his group

Sutter's Fort with Sutter's Indian soldiers. The American flag has just replaced the Mexican flag.
*Colonized. **From: SAMCC***

separated, then killed most of his men and left him in the wilderness without food or guns. Later, in Nevada, other Indians saved his life by bringing him food and water when he was almost dead. Almost 200 years ago when only Indians and wild animals lived here, Jedediah came to the American River area twice. The Bike Path that is named for him follows much of the same trail he walked. He would have seen the same cliffs and the ancestors of some of the same plants.

After Jedediah's second visit, he went north to Fort Vancouver, western headquarters for the Hudson's Bay Company. Smith's valuable supply of beaver pelts was just what the Canadians were looking for. Profits from beaver fur were so important in the development of Canada that to this day the beaver is a symbol of Canada. The Hudson's Bay Com-

and their hunting killed many of the large animals.

A few years before Sutter, one of the first Americans in California almost started Sacramento when John Cooper asked the Mexican governor to give him land along the American River. Cooper called the river "Rio Ojotska" which is Russian for "hunter". Cooper knew the Russians at Fort Ross north of San Francisco and that's what they called the river since hunters from many nations loved the area. The governor granted Cooper the land, as always ignoring the fact that Indians had lived there for thousands of years. Cooper decided he would rather live near his Russian friends and settled for a ranch north of San Francisco.

pany immediately began sending beaver trapping expeditions into California.

From Jedediah Smith's first visits in 1827 until after John Sutter begin building his fort in 1839, more than ten trapping parties passed through the Sacramento area, unintentionally bringing death. These trappers carried diseases which killed most of the Indians in this area

In 1837 the American River was given its current name by Governor Alvarado, who called it the "Rio do los Americanos" because the area was full of "trappers of revolutionary proclivities." The Mexicans were worried that the Americans would want to be free of their rule. They were right.

The Spanish had been searching for gold in the New World for 300 years. They never found the richest strike of all in California. **Photo: Tom Meyers**

J ohn Sutter traveled up the Sacramento River from San Francisco on a small sailing ship captained by William Davis and landed on the south bank of the American in August 1839 near what later became 28th and B streets in Sacramento. Alone at night with his small crew on the banks of a river wilderness, Sutter could hear Indians sneaking up on his camp. Frightened, he made the wise decision to fire his small cannon at a tree across the river, not at the Indians. When the Indians saw the tree splinter, they decided not to attack.

If Sutter had fired directly at the Indians, he might have killed a few, but the rest could have attacked for revenge.

Instead the Indians helped him choose a place above the floods. They worked for him building a fort and ranch that would become the welcoming place in California for settlers from the far away eastern United States. Sutter was out to make money, but in doing so he learned he could do better with cooperation than fighting. He worked with the Mexicans, bought Fort Ross from the Russians and gave shelter to weary American pioneers. He set the business tone for what Sacramento would become: supply center to the Gold Rush and, eventually, capital of the richest state in the richest country in the world.

In the mean time, it was a beautiful country.

An early visitor reported:

The ground is trodden up by immense herds of cattle and horses which grazed here in the early spring, when it was wet and apparently miry. We passed through large evergreen oak groves, some of them miles in width. Game is very abundant. We frequently saw deer feeding quietly one or two hundred yards from us, and large flocks of antelope.

(Edwin Bryant, 1846)

In addition to Sutter, other pioneers got huge land grants from the Mexican government. These were broken up after a few years and sold to settlers.

One of the best descriptions of the Sacramento area before the Gold Rush was written by John Fremont, an American army officer and explorer called "The Great Pathfinder":

March 1. We are rapidly descending into the spring and we are leaving our snowy region far behind; everything is getting green; butterflies are swarming; numerous bugs are creeping out, wakened from their winter's sleep, and the forest flowers are coming into bloom.

*March 3. At every step the country improved in beauty; the pines were rapidly disappearing and the oaks became the principal trees of the forest...
In a short distance we crossed a little*

rivulet, where two old huts stood, and nearby were heaps of acorn hulls. The ground round about was very rich, covered with an exuberant sward of grass.

March 4. We encamped in the evening on the shore of the river, at a place where the associated beauties of scenery made so strong an impression on us that we have given it the name Beautiful Camp (probably Coloma, within sight of the spot where gold would be discovered four years latter).

March 6. We continued on our road, through the same surpassingly beautiful country, entirely unequalled for the pasturage of stock by anything we had ever seen ... The valley being gay with flowers, and some of the banks being absolutely golden with California poppy.

March 8. We encamped at the junction of the two rivers, the Sacramento and the American, in the beautiful valley of Sacramento. **(John Fremont, 1844)**

Fremont's map maker was scared because he got lost from Fremont near the upper American River:

February 29. Under the circumstances, I feel quite satisfied in this magnificent spring weather and mountain air. The water gurgles at my feet; green trees, live oaks and many kinds of conifers all around.

March 1. The path is slippery because of the dry fir needles. What weather. Everything has started to sprout. Butterflies fly about, also mosquitoes, beetles and ants. Everything is alive.

March 2. The eternal going up and down hill is so exhausting that I'd rather camp here by the water at a good fire and suffer a little hunger than to continue to run around in these rocks and mountains.

March 3. This is beginning to get serious. I couldn't find the others and I am here alone. Since yesterday morning I have not eaten a thing except a few (wild) sweet onions which I just scratched out of the ground. At the same time, I found an ant's nest, a portion of which I bit off and swallowed. Nor do I have any tobacco. How will this end?

(Charles Pruess, 1844)

It ended just fine. Fremont found him and they all made it back safely.

Most of the settlers were in their teens or 20's. It was a long hard journey.
They missed their homes and friends. **From: SEP, Hough**

Into the Mountains.

The land was flat most of the way across the United States.

When the going got steep and dangerous, settlers risked their families and everything they owned in a mountain world most of them had never even seen before.

From: CSL

Chapter Four
CONQUEST OF CALIFORNIA

**We are a marvel to ourselves
and a miracle to the world...**
*Peter Burnett, First American
Governor of California*

People often loved California once they got there, but getting to California in pioneer times was about as easy as going to the North Pole. Most pioneers walked and rode horses for six months across dangerous country to get to California by wagon train. There were no planes or trains, so the only other way to go was a long way around on a ship.

Travelers could sail for six months around the bottom of South America through rough seas almost all the way to the South Pole. Some people risked a short cut across the jungles of Central America which might cut the journey to two months, if they didn't die along the way. California felt far from home; even years later, many emigrants had their tombstones carved with the name of the state they came from back East. In California, many people felt as though they were living beyond the edge of the real world.

It might have been far away, but California was the place where there was room to make money and raise a family. People thought that the United States had what they called a Manifest Destiny: the country was so great it just had to cover the whole continent from the Atlantic to the Pacific. When people wrote home about California, local newspapers would often print their descriptions of a beautiful land. That made more Americans decide to risk the long trip west.

Settlers

In the years after Fremont found the path, overland emigrants in the 1840s and 1850s usually ended up moving their tired wagon trains down the mountain trails to Sacramento. For thousands of people, Sutter's Fort was the first outpost of civilization they had seen in months. The sight of the adobe-walled fort meant that the hardship and danger were finally over.

Sutter tried to help, but he was overwhelmed:

At times my buildings were filled with emigrants. So much so that I could scarcely find a spot to lay my own head to rest.

My farm-house and store-houses were filled every winter during these immigration times with poor, wet, hungry men, women and children seeking a fortune in a new land. They were of my breed and they loved the promise of the soil. Often it was necessary for me to go with my men and cattle to drag them into safety out of the snow. These poor usually arrived in a destitute condition and hard indeed would have been the man who demanded payment for shelter, food, or clothing.

Very few possessed more than their teams when they arrived. They came to my Fort with nothing but their tired bodies and their rain wet clothing.

(John Sutter, 1855)

The Donner Party

It could cost as much to outfit a wagon for the California trip as it did to buy a house. One of the richest and best equipped wagon trains had the worst trouble. The Donner party of 80 people started across the mountains in 1846 too close to winter time and got trapped. The snow drifts were 20 feet high, way over their heads.

Starving, they ate everything they had, in the end even some dead bodies. Hungry adults and children died before rescuers from Sutter's Fort and other places below the snow pushed their way through to save the ones who were still alive.

Virginia Reed was 13 years old:

I would cry and wish I had what you all wasted... we had to kill little Cash the dog and eat him - [they left Martha Patty 8 and Thomas 3 behind and went to look for their dad bringing help] - that was the hardest thing yet, to come on and leave them there... Martha said, well Ma, if you never see me again, do the best you can. The men said they could hardly stand it, it made them all cry... We went over great high mountains in snow up to our knees. Little James [5 years old] walked the whole way over all the mountain in snow up to his waist. He said every step he took he was getting closer to Pa and something to eat...When we had traveled five days, we met Pa... you do not know how glad we were to see him.

The whole Reed family survived and went on to make money from both gold mining and farming. Not everyone was that tough and lucky; 36 people died including two Nisenan Indian boys who were trying to guide the Donner party to safety.

You can see the spot where they were trapped in Donner Memorial Park at the eastern end of Donner Lake. The doll that 8 year old Martha Patty Reed carried all the way is still in Sutter's Fort.

Martha Patty Reed's doll survived the Donner Party.
It is now in Sutter's Fort.

At this same time, American settlers in the Sacramento Valley decided to get rid of the Mexican officials, before the Mexicans carried out a plan to get rid of the Americans. They started the Bear Flag revolt and marched on the Mexican General Vallejo's ranch in Sonoma in 1846.

Settlers captured Mexican General Mariano Vallejo and declared the independent Republic of California. Vallejo was so nice that when the settlers came with guns he invited them in for a drink and they forgot to tell him the bad news until hours later. The Americans took Vallejo to Sutter's Fort and held him prisoner for two months. After his release Vallejo returned to Sonoma and burned his Mexican uniforms. He actually thought that becoming part of America might be a good thing.

In the Mexican California capital of Monterey, the United States Navy stormed ashore and raised the American flag.

Early settler John Bidwell wrote:

We simply marched all over California from Sonoma to San Diego and raised the American flag without [much] opposition or protest. We tried to find an enemy but, could not.

44

When the takeover started, Fremont was camped along the American River eight or ten miles from the river's mouth, probably in the vicinity of the present Howe Avenue Bridge. Fremont took command of Sutter's Fort. Sutter wanted to be the boss of the Sacramento Valley, but now he had to do what the Americans said, even in his own fort.

Even so, Sutter was happy. It looked like he was finally going to make some money. He had trees cut in the foothills and rafted down the American to build a flour mill. But he needed a saw mill to cut the trees into boards. Fortunately, among the handful of Americans living in the area was a carpenter named James Marshall. Sutter and Marshall agreed to be partners and build a saw mill. Marshall knew the perfect spot for the mill. It was in a valley on the American River both the Indians and the explorers said was beautiful.

They called it Coloma.

You have just stepped off a riverboat into Old Sacramento early in the Gold Rush. Sam Brannan's store on the right is ready to sell you that shovel you forgot for what would be $300 in modern money—take it or leave it, there was no place else to shop. The City Hotel on the left is the best and almost only hotel in town-- with canvas walls and that shaky gangplank over muddy Front Street. The Eagle Theatre to the middle has wild plays (see Chapter 7 under Entertainment). Between the Eagle and Brannan's you can see the Round Tent Saloon where the booze and gambling never stop. Prices are high (see Chapter 6 under Expensive California), but you have been passing men in this picture who have just come back with thousands of dollars in nuggets from the gold country, a day's ride beyond the trees that cover most of Sacramento.

Colorized from Gold Rush drawing: SAMCC

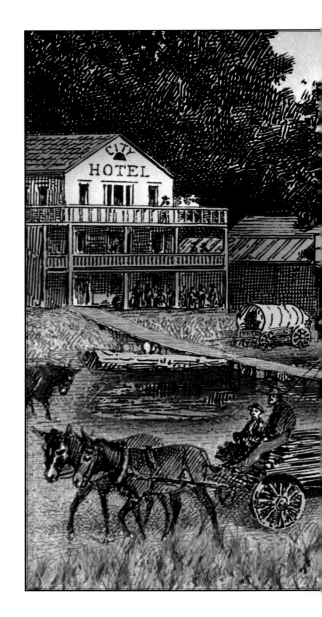

Chapter Five
THE GOLD RUSH

It tingled in the ear and at the finger-ends; it buzzed about the brain and tickled in the stomach; it warmed the blood and swelled the heart; new fires were kindled on the hearth-stones, new castles builded in the air.
Hubert Howe Bancroft
Gold Miner and Historian

A 14 year old boy, by himself, finds gold. **Photo: Noel Neuburger.**

A 14-year-old boy mining by himself for a couple of months brought home $70,000 in modern dollars.

There was enough gold in California to live like a king. One man dug up 11 pounds (worth $50,000 today) in three days and his friends took turns digging until they all had enough. People believed if they had courage in their hearts, they could travel for thousands of miles and work in icy mountain streams to uncover treasure. Many people found their dreams, although often more from the adventure than from the gold. The Gold Rush that changed the world was centered in the Sacramento area and the riches in history and adventure have never left.

The western United States was the only place in the world free enough to have a Gold Rush: in any other country the gold would have been claimed by rich land owners or the government. California became part of the United States on almost the same winter day in 1848 that gold was discovered by people building a saw mill on the American River near Sacramento. There were no rich land owners yet and no real government.

The Gold Rush was a tidal wave of people sweeping across the most valuable new land the world had ever found. San Francisco went from a quiet village to a famous seaport literally built over the top of hundreds of ships abandon by gold hungry sailors. Sacramento, the jumping-off place for the mines, expanded from a muddy landing to the hub of a golden wheel that included Placerville, Auburn, Yuba City and Grass Valley.

Sutter was almost trampled by the rush. He had a town laid out, just south of the present Sacramento zoo, modestly named Sutterville. Nobody wanted to live there. The Gold Rush crowds settled around the landing in what is now Old Sacramento where the banks were high enough to unload a ship. A city of tents and shacks sprang up, was flooded and rebuilt; burned and rose again; there were riots, lynching, more floods and epidemics, yet through it all Sacramento and the Gold Country just kept growing. It took more than 200 years for the United States to reach the Missouri River and only a year to jump that far again to California.

In January 1848, James Marshall was up early working on

A prospector looking for "color", very carefully.   Once some gold was found, he would bring in a long tom for faster sorting.
Photo: Tom Meyers

the saw mill he and Sutter were building on the American River in Coloma. He saw "something shining in the bottom of the ditch":

. . .after shutting off the water from the race I stepped into it, near the lower end, and there upon the rock, about six inches beneath the surface of the water, I discovered the gold. . .

I was entirely alone at the time. I picked up one or two pieces and examined them attentively; having some general knowledge of minerals, I could not call to mind more than two which in any way resembled this—sulphuret of iron, very bright and brittle; and gold, bright, yet malleable (bendable).

I then tried it between two rocks and found that it could be beaten into a different shape, but not broken...

I went to the Fort... and carried with me about three ounces of the gold, which Capt. Sutter and I tested.

Sutter looked up gold in an encyclopedia. After doing tests the book recommended, he was sure they had the real thing.

John Sutter saw the discovery as a threat. He had big plans for an empire at Sacramento and was not ready for the world to rush in. Hoping to keep the gold secret, Sutter rode up into the hills along the American River to Coloma where he spoke with his workers:

I told them that I would consider it as a great favor if they would keep this discovery secret for only six weeks, so that I could finish my large flour mill at Brighton, which had cost me already from 24 to 25,000 dollars [almost half a million dollars in modern money]—the people up there promised to keep it a secret ...

On my way home, instead of feeling happy and contented, I was unhappy, and could not see that it could benefit me much...

He might have been worried, but Sutter himself helped spread the news. He rented the gold discovery site at Coloma from the local Indians and sent a messenger to Monterey asking the military governor, Colonel R. B. Mason, to approve the lease. With the messenger, Sutter sent six ounces of gold nuggets worth more than $2,000 in modern money.

Even though Sutter's secret leaked out, people didn't start to stampede into the Sierras, yet. Rumors of gold had circulated in California for years. Juan Alvarado even made rings for his family from small amounts of gold found in the San Jose area around 1838.

But this was different.

It took a clever Mormon, Sam Brannan, to stir up the stampede. Brannan had a store at Sutter's Fort and it didn't take him long to figure out what was happening. Quietly Brannan began buying up every pick, pan and shovel he could find. When his gold mining supplies were safely at his store ready to sell, Brannan went to San Francisco. He printed newspapers with the exciting news of gold. Four months after the discovery, with hat in one hand and a bottle of gold dust in the other, Brannan ran through the streets, yelling:

"Gold! Gold! Gold from the American River!"

Great Excitement

The Result was electric. Said one future miner:

I looked on for a moment; a frenzy seized my soul; unbidden my legs performed some entirely new movements of polka steps—I took several—houses were too small for me to stay in; I was soon in the street in search of necessary outfits; piles of gold rose up before me at every step; castles of marble, dazzling the eye with their rich appliances; thousands of slaves bowing to my beck and call; myriads of fair virgins contending with each other for my love—were among the fancies of my fevered imagination. The Rothschilds, Girards, and Astors appeared to me but poor people; in short, I had a very violent attack of gold fever.

The few thousand settlers already in California were excited, but back east people thought it was just more western tall tales. Months went by and finally the westerners sent back a tea box stuffed with 230 ounces of pure California gold, almost $100,000 in modern money. That convinced the President. His message to Congress at the end of year set off the biggest stampede in the history of the world: the California Gold Rush.

During the year before the good news spread, there was more gold than Californians to dig it up. Sailors jumped overboard to head for the hills; ships could not leave San Francisco because there was not enough crew left to set the sails. Both Sutter and his neighbor John Sinclair used Indians who did not even have pans or shovels; they filtered

Miners working together with a long tom.
From: BP.

river rocks through their hand-made baskets.

During the first year there were more natives mining for gold than settlers, although the Indians did not get to keep what they found. Through the hard work of his natives, Sinclair made almost half a million dollars in modern money during the first few months. As he feared, John Sutter's empire was overrun:

As soon as the secret was out my labor-ers began to leave me, in small parties at first, but then all left, from the clerk to the cook...

What a great misfortune was this sud-den gold discovery for me. It had just broken up and ruined my hard, rest-less and industrious labors, connected

with many danger of life, as I had many narrow escapes before I became properly established.

There is a saying that men will steal everything but a milestone and a mill-stone. They stole my millstones...
The country swarmed with lawless men. I was alone...

At first, prospectors stayed around the streams uphill from Sacramento. When gold was discovered to the north and south, treasure seekers began to believe that there had once been a golden volcano that blew a "Mother Lode" of molten yellow metal over the foothills. Ten men working together made $30,000 each in modern money in less

54

than two weeks. One person digging in a small hole the size of a sink found two and a half pounds of gold, more than $11,000 worth in modern money in 15 minutes. From South American to China, young people felt the pull of the golden mountain. Most of the gold was still there, waiting...

Where Gold Comes From

Gold comes from the stars. It was formed before the earth cooled into a planet. It has been found in small quantities all over the earth, but in large amounts only in a few places. The Sierra Nevada both north and south of Sacramento has been some of the richest gold country in the world.

Gold is valuable because it is useful, beautiful and rare. All the gold ever found in the entire world could be stacked on one football field. It does not rust; a gold ring made in the time of Caesar still looks new today. It does not break, even when stretched very thin: one ounce of gold can be pulled into a wire 40 miles long. It is twice as heavy as lead; a solid gold basketball would weigh over half a ton. Gold helped make America rich, California gold totals more than 40 billion dollars. In the 25 years after gold was discovered on the American River; more gold was

mined around the world than in the 350 years before.

Sierra Nevada gold is mostly placer gold, occurring on the surface in or around streams. There is more: buried veins of gold run for miles underground. Gold that was brought to the surface came from hundreds of millions of years of slow earth movement and sometimes by violent volcano explosions.

Three hundred million years ago, the Sacramento area was underwater, part of a huge lake that covered the whole Central Valley. Fish swam where millions people now live. Then about 130 million years ago, way before any people lived here, volcanoes begin to push solid rock up to become the Sierra Nevada mountains.

As the rock cracked open, liquid gold and other minerals welled upward from the earth's molten interior. Over millions of years, erosion slowly wore away the rock. As some gold veins were exposed, small particles of the gold were carried away, mostly in flakes but occasionally in nuggets the size of a finger or even a fist. Glistening gold tumbled down the mountain streams to be found in sand bars and gravel beds. Sometimes a vein of gold led way underground. Either way, a lucky miner might find more treasure than he could earn in a lifetime of work.

How to mine gold

People like to dream about finding a nugget of pure gold. It has happened: one miner found a piece of gold as long as a football by the American River near Auburn in the Sacramento foothills. However, most gold comes mixed up with other rocks. The glittering metal can either be loose with river sand and gravel (called placer mining) or inside bigger rocks underground (quartz mining).

Even still today, prospecting miners use a kind of big pie pan which has a flat bottom and sides that slope outward. They take gravel from a high water location or a dry old stream bed and carefully shake or rotate the pan, floating away sand while the gold (if any) settles in the bottom of the pan. Stones are raked out by hand. Panning takes time, 15 minutes to make sure all the gold is gathered from each pan.

Once miners found gold,

Gold Miners came from all over the world.
From CSL.

they built a simple wooden trough to wash the treasure so they could go through more river bottom than would fit in a pan. Sand and gravel, hopefully containing gold, was shoveled into the trough or sluice box with plenty of water. Riffle boards at the bottom of the box caught the heavy gold while lighter gravel and sand were washed away.

The bigger the sluice box and the more water, the more gravel could be sifted for gold.

dug in the ground. The rest of the mountain washed down hill, clogging rivers and burying houses. Hydraulic mining made lots of money, but at a terrible cost to the earth. Damage to everyone downstream eventually led California judges to issue the first environmental court order in the world, banning uncontained hydraulic mining.

When the gold was inside quartz rocks underground, the only way to get it was to tunnel. Miners dug down to a vein of gold and then followed it, no matter how deep it went, drilling into the rock and blasting tunnels underground. Some of these tunnels went for miles under the earth.

Sometimes gold is found in a dry stream bed that hasn't seen water for thousands of years. To get water to all the places they could wash out gold, miners worked together to build narrow canals many miles long. Some of these canals or miner's ditches still carry water to Gold Country homes.

Where there was a lot of water, hydraulic mining used huge water nozzles to blast away mountain sides, with the gold bearing rocks caught in troughs

After a blast, miners would try to knock down all the loose hanging rocks with long steel pry bars so that one of these "widowmakers" would not fall and crush them. It was hard work digging deep underground, even more unnerving when tunnel blasting explosions rocked the dark shafts. Miners brought up millions of dollars of gold ore in small rail cars often pulled by mules who never saw the light of day.

Golden Cities

Most of the billions of (modern) dollars in treasure came from the foothills, but miners even panned for gold in the dirt streets of Sacramento city following a flood. Soon after they discovered gold at Coloma a few miles outside of Placerville, John Sutter's workers found a treasure trove near what is now Folsom. Since gold is 19 times heavier than water, it settles when the river slows down. The place where the forks of the American join coming out of the foothills near Sacramento was a natural goldfield.

An incredibly rich gravel bar about as long as a football field became the center of a city called Mormon Island, now submerged under Folsom Lake. Sam Brannan, Mormon leader and dedicated money-maker, opened a store and began a free ferry service. Within a month, four miners left for Los Angeles with 100 pounds of gold (worth $500,000 in today's money).

*On the left, the Pelton wheel-- first real improvement in the waterwheel in 1,000 years, invented in Gold Country. To the right, a stamp mill for smashing rocks to look for gold. **Photo: Tom Meyers.***

For the first years of the Gold Rush, Mormon Island was like a natural bank. Miners arriving in Sacramento without money went to Mormon Island hoping to find enough gold to pay their way to the foothills. As befits a golden bank, Mormon Island was not cheap. The fare, one way, on California's first stage line from Sacramento to the Island was two ounces of gold (more than $700 in modern money). Broke miners walked the 25 miles. If they struck it rich they could afford tickets to the fabulous Christmas ball of 1849, twenty dollars then, $400 in today's money.

Sam Brannan collected a 10 percent tithe from the Mormon miners and rent from non-Mormons. He apparently decided that money was more important than his religion. When a messenger from the Mormon church arrived and announced that "the Lord wants his tithe", Sam replied that the Lord could have his offering when the Lord provided Sam with a signed receipt.

A fire destroyed most of Mormon Island a few years into the Gold Rush and people moved to the growing railroad town of Folsom a few miles south.

Modern residents drive down the road everyday without knowing that they are passing former treasure sites once full of gold.

Years before the Gold Rush a fur trader asked John Sutter what the best place would be to do business with the Indians. Sutter suggested the natural ford across the American at present-day Folsom. The trader set out but stopped a few miles short, camping on a large sand bar on the north side of the river upstream from where Fair Oaks and the Hazel Avenue bridge are now. He named the bar for his home state, Mississippi. No one knows how much money he made trading beads for furs, but it wouldn't have seemed like enough if he had found out after he left that he had been camping right on top of gold, a strike called Mississippi Bar.

Sailor Bar upstream from Sunrise Avenue was mined by crew from some of the more than 300 vessels left stranded in San Francisco Bay. They were so anxious to get to the gold that some of them jumped overboard before their ships even landed. A daring project called the

American River Ditch carried water from the mountains 39 miles to Sailor and Mississippi bars, where the water washed gold and was eventually returned to the river. Most of the miners probably did not even know that they were digging up the site of a village that had been the home of Indians for hundreds of years. With still more gold to get, in the early 20th century these gravel bars were one of many locations along the American River mined by dredgers.

Negro Bar

Negro Bar was on the south bank of the American across from Negro Bar State Park, a few steps from what is now Folsom's old town. African-Americans discovered gold here early in the Gold Rush.

By the middle of 1850, the men who gave Negro Bar its name moved upstream four miles to Negro Hill, where gold was being mined by an African American minister. People of different races lived and worked together in this area for years. Their peace was marred in 1855 when drunken white men invaded the African American section of Negro Hill and killed a man. They were arrested and tried, but later released. Since it was against the law in early California for African Americans, Indians and Chinese to testify against whites in court, it was often hard to get a conviction in racial crimes.

Working against prejudice, people with African American heritage contributed to the growth of California. Peter Ranne was with Jedediah Smith on the first American cross county exploration to California. Mountain man and guide James Beckwourth knew trails from Florida to San Francisco, got to the gold fields before the 49ers and has a mountain pass named after him. William Leidesdorff owned 35,000 acres of land south of the American River, including Negro Bar and what became the town of Folsom. A successful businessman for years before the Gold Rush, Leidesdorff brought the first steamship to the San Francisco Bay, donated land for schools in San Francisco and was vice consul of the United States in California.

In 1851 the entire American

River was turned out of its channel at Negro Bar following a year of cooperative dam and ditch building by almost 300 miners. After all that work, the exposed bed of the river didn't pay off the way they had hoped. The miners moved on, leaving this less productive area to mostly Chinese prospectors. As Folsom grew with the coming of the railroad, it took over the all the business and Negro Bar faded away.

Golden Lessons

Gold Rush miners might strike it rich, but they were far more likely to work hard, have some wild times and wind up broke. Miners were mostly men from 18 to 25; women were so rare in the early days that a miner once gave the first girl he saw a gold nugget just so he could talk to her. Prospectors who made money had lots of help spending it; gold towns had plenty of bar stools, gambling tables and dance halls. Said one visitor to a Sacramento casino:

At times these little tables are literally covered with buckskin bags filled with gold dust. Thousands and thousands of dollars change hands every hour from morning until late in the night.

They called it "seeing the elephant", a great adventure that would leave them wiser if not richer. They called themselves "Argonauts" after Greek voyagers who discovered new lands while sailing after gold at the beginning of western civilization. Most of the hundreds of thousands of treasure seekers had never been more than 20 miles from their homes before they set off on their journey of 3,000 miles or more.

Said Forty-Niner John Hittell:

The people who come to California are bold adventurers naturally. We were dissatisfied with life in Europe and the Eastern states, because it was too slow. We came here to enjoy an exciting life and make money rapidly... It is no uncommon thing to see men who have been wealthy on three or four different occasions and then poor again... When men fail they do not despair... they hope to be rich again.

The Gold Rush was years before the Civil War, a time when slavery was still legal in much of the United States. Archy Lee was brought to Sacramento as a slave and freed by the California courts. His attorney was Edwin Crocker who would later help his brother and partners Stan-

The El Dorado Hotel bar. Gold mining was such a gamble that actual gambling seemed like a natural activity, especially with the free lunch and cheap drinks. Gambling was the last chance to make a fortune and the first chance to lose it. From: CSL.

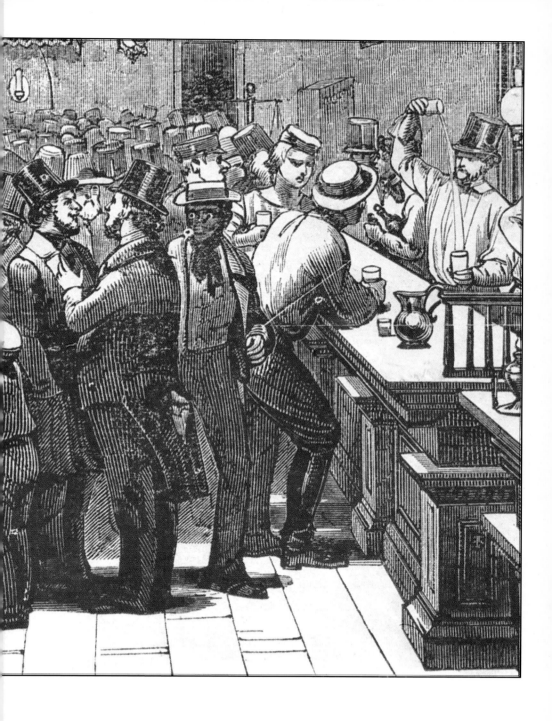

ford, Huntington and Hartford build the transcontinental railroad to Sacramento. These local Sacramento store keepers cared about something besides money --they got to know each other at anti-slavery meetings of the early California Republican party. Gold Rush Californians had the prejudice of their times against Indians, Mexicans, Chinese and African Americans; but as contradictory as it was, they also believe in freedom. Tons of gold and silver from the west helped the Union win the Civil War.

The Gold Rush idea that anybody could become rich stood out like a Sierra sunrise against the old eastern ideas of inherited wealth and social class. When Jefferson wrote about "life, liberty and the pursuit of happiness" 75 years before the Gold Rush, most people were stuck where their parents had been. For better and sometimes worse, the Gold Rush that was born in Sacramento and the Gold Country helped make the pursuit of happiness real.

To The Gold!

The bigger the golden blob on the map, the more gold was discovered. You probably won't get rich, but there is still gold to find!

NEVADA CITY

GRASS VALLEY

YUBA CITY
MARYSVILLE

49

AUBURN

COLOMA
(GOLD DISCOVERY)

80

ROSEVILLE

PLACERVILLE
(HANGTOWN)

FOLSOM

FAIR OAKS
50

SACRAMENTO

SHINGLE SPRINGS

ELK GROVE

5

SUTTER CREEK

- A Klondike gold pan has high sides and riffles to help catch the gold.
- Scoop sand and gravel into the pan from a high water location, dry old stream bed or the downstream side of a boulder.
- Swish water around in the pan, floating away sand while the gold (if any) settles to the bottom. Clear out stones with your fingers.
- Take your time; 15 minutes if you see a glow.

- Gold is the same color as a wedding ring and usually in flakes mixed with sand.
- Black sand (iron) is often near gold.
- Once in a great while, people find a whole rock or nugget of gold.
- Real gold flattens when you hit it, fools gold breaks.

Chapter Six
AFTER THE GOLD RUSH

**When we came here, about six weeks ago,
there were only one or two tents in sight, and in one short week,
our tent is in the center of town, with six stores, two blacksmith
shops, drug stores, taverns, bakery, circus, et cetera.
Verily, California is a go-ahead country.**
Auburn Ravine miner
John Eagle, 1852

As the years went by, the Gold Rush changed from a treasure hunt into a business. In the first 10 years of the rush, California mined gold worth $10,000,000,000 in current dollars. Most people did not get rich but many managed to keep a few dollars to buy a home or start a business. During the Gold Rush, the residents of California produced wealth at a rate twenty times higher than any other state. As time went by, independent prospectors gave up trying to strike it rich in the icy streams of the high canyons and found a sure income in factories, stores and mines run by companies.

Even though Oregon had good land, ten times as many people moved to California. They were drawn by high pay as much as by hope for gold. A Sacramento waiter or carpenter could make twice as much as he could back east. Fortunes were possible for people with enough nerve or money to open their own business. A widow lady north of Auburn made the modern equivalent of a third of a million dollars just by baking pies. Stores, hotels, even farming in the right place at the right time could make millions. There was freedom to try something new.

As one writer said: *"There is nothing around us older than ourselves."*

Said another: *"Recklessness is in the air...The roaring winds off the Pacific make you drunk with it..."*

People thought of clever ways to reach for golden profits. One small company of investors in the southern mines built a diving bell to pick up gold underwater.

To The Gold!

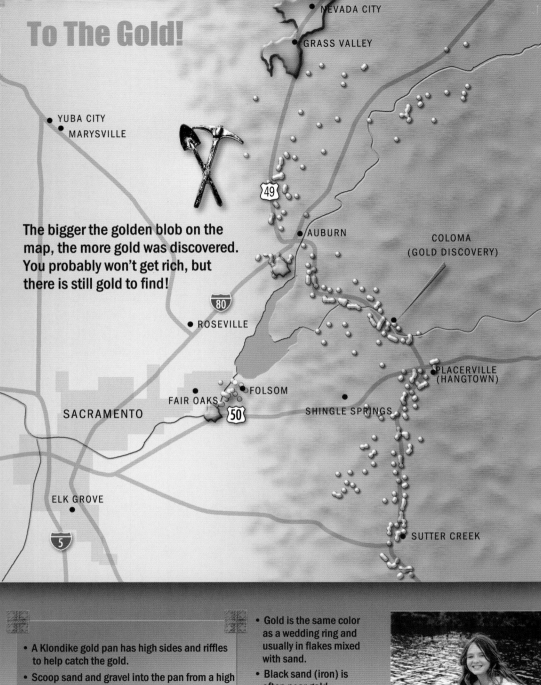

The bigger the golden blob on the map, the more gold was discovered. You probably won't get rich, but there is still gold to find!

NEVADA CITY

GRASS VALLEY

YUBA CITY
MARYSVILLE

49

AUBURN

COLOMA
(GOLD DISCOVERY)

80

ROSEVILLE

PLACERVILLE
(HANGTOWN)

FOLSOM

FAIR OAKS

SACRAMENTO

50

SHINGLE SPRINGS

ELK GROVE

SUTTER CREEK

5

- A Klondike gold pan has high sides and riffles to help catch the gold.
- Scoop sand and gravel into the pan from a high water location, dry old stream bed or the downstream side of a boulder.
- Swish water around in the pan, floating away sand while the gold (if any) settles to the bottom. Clear out stones with your fingers.
- Take your time; 15 minutes if you see a glow.

- Gold is the same color as a wedding ring and usually in flakes mixed with sand.
- Black sand (iron) is often near gold.
- Once in a great while, people find a whole rock or nugget of gold.
- Real gold flattens when you hit it, fools gold breaks.

It sprang a leak. Miners changed the course of rivers so they could search for gold on the dried up river bed. In one river once the water was gone, several boulders that weighed as much as elephants stood in their way. The miners didn't have any dynamite so they built a huge fire around the boulders and kept it going for hours. When the boulders were red hot, they sent the icy river back over them. The boulders cracked, the miners moved the pieces, and underneath was a bonanza of gold.

In the early 1850's a vein of gold 18 inches thick was discovered near Grass Valley. Miners could hit a rock with a hammer and pieces of gold would fall out. Nearby miners noticed that rocks they had used to build their cabin looked the same, so they spent months breaking apart their fireplace and chimney and made more than half a million dollars in today's money. When a single golden nugget weighing 14 pounds was displayed at the first world's fair in London's Crystal Palace, rich British investors became eager to finance quartz mines that dug deep into the earth to follow the rich vein.

Hydraulic Mining

In 1855 a new mining technique was devised that was good at getting gold but bad for everything else: hydraulic mining used high pressure water to blast into the ground. Ironically, it was the only totally new way of getting gold discovered during the Gold Rush. Operations were modest in the beginning, with nozzles like big garden hoses shooting a stream of water against a gravel bank. The run-off was channeled into a ditch or box which collected gold in riffles, making it a non-stop sluice.

After years of small scale hydraulic mining, an inventor in Marysville came up with the monitor, a giant water gun that could wash away hillsides -- rocks, trees, boulders and all.

Said the state mineralogist:
"If a giant nozzle should be set in front of the strongest building in San Francisco and a stream turned on it, the walls would melt away in a few minutes."

The monitor required huge amounts of water. Gold hungry miners built 5,000 miles of canals and aqueducts to carry water for this liquid artillery. Watching a monitor in action was an awe-

Less than 10 years from being a muddy riverbank, Sacramento was the world famous capital of California with the first railroad in the west proudly steaming in from Folsom near the top of this amazingly detailed picture called City of the Plain. **From SAMCC, Baker 1857**

some sight:

With a rumble like thunder rolling close in the mountains, the giant monitor swung in a lowering arc, sending a stream of tortured water into the rubble of dirt and boulders, cascading a flow of mud and debris down into the sturdy riffle boxes and through a tunnel out of the hydraulic pit down the precipitous chasm in whose bottom the American River glimmered.
(Grass Valley-Nevada City Union)

Riding an hydraulic mining nozzle powerful enough to knock down a building or blast away a hillside. **From: SAMCC.**

Hydraulic mining was destructive but also profitable. One company in three months used three and a half billion gallons of water, enough to fill every bathtub in the United State today. The company washed one million cubic yards of placer gravel and took out $576,000 in today's money in gold. Unfortunately, to get this money, the soil just this one company washed away in 100 days would have covered an area the size of downtown Sacramento with mud four inches thick. And there were lots of companies. One company used almost 70,000 gallons of water for each twenty modern dollars in gold recovered.

By 1879 the number of ditches had increased to 640, with a total length of 6,585 miles; enough to stretch across the United States twice. These ditches delivered more than four billion gallons of water for gold mining each day. This is more water than is used by the total of every California home for everything today.

The miners recovered only the gold. There was no way to hold back the accompanying soil and rocks from the mines, called "slickens", which slowly washed down the stream beds

Farmers whose carefully tended crops were buried alive called hydraulic mining: *"an evil to be stopped at once, either by law or gunfire".*

The state engineer estimated in 1878 that 18,000 acres of valley land on the Yuba, once the choicest in the state, had been buried beneath mining debris. The mining companies claimed that technology would solve the problem, but the log dams they built to try to hold back the slickens were quickly buried.

Once their homes and businesses were threatened, Sacramento's County Board of Supervisors sent the sheriff to stop the Gold Run Ditch and Mining Company. This company was beginning to blast away on the north fork of the American River and slickens were already oozing down stream. Sacramento was trapped between mining mud from the Sacramento River on one side and the American River on the other.

into the river valleys where people lived and grew food. River rose and threatened Sacramento, Marysville, Yuba City and all the towns and farms around with drowning.

The water of the Sacramento River overflowed its high banks to a depth of 6 inches in 1849-50; 12 inches in 1853-54; 2 feet in 1861-62; 3 1/2 feet in 1867-68; and 5 feet in 1877-78. The city was flooded, but riverboats got stuck on washed down mud before they even got close to town.

The legal case went on for seven months with heated arguments on both sides from hundreds of experts. Then in 1882, Judge Temple granted a

Miners headed as much as two miles underground. Empire Mine, Grass Valley.
From SAMCC

Ditch and Mining company. This company was beginning to blast away on the north fork of the American River and slickens were already oozing down stream. Sacramento was trapped between mining mud from the Sacramento River on one side and the American River on the other.

The legal case went on for seven months with heated arguments on both sides from hundreds of experts. Then in 1882, Judge Temple granted a permanent injuction prohibiting the company from depositing depositing "coarse" debris in the American River:

I have concluded to so find that when the heavier debris is completely impounded, mining may be resumed, virtually refusing to hold that the plaintiff (Sacramento Board of Supervisors) may enjoin such operations as only corrupt the water with mud and render it less suitable for domestic and other uses.

Perhaps I am somewhat moved to this by the consideration that otherwise mining can never be prosecuted at all... I confess I shrink from the consequence so far-reaching.

(People vs. Gold Run Ditch and Mining Company)

beautiful American River began to cloud up with hydraulic debris. It lived under a death sentence: there were plans for massive hydraulic mining that could bury the American forever.

At first, nobody wanted to do anything. Hydraulic mining turned out 90 percent of the gold in California. Mining was a major industry and source of jobs. But the Board of Supervisors sent the sheriff to stop the Gold Run

The digging part of a dredger.
From SAMCC

their claim to be first and most valuable would win the day. Besides, the judge who heard the case had started out as a 49er, prospecting for gold with a pick and shovel along the same streams the miners were now blasting.

The case took almost two years. The miner turned judge listened to 200 witnesses and made personal trips to look at both the hydraulic mines and the flooded valley towns and farms. When the judge sat down to give his decision, California held its breath. He read for three and a half hours, citing experience and legal precedent. At the end, his decision was clear: no one has the right to cause mining pollution which damages the life and property of other people. Miners were legally forbidden from dumping any kind of debris, coarse or fine, big or small, into the rivers. From Stockton all the way to Red Bluff, valley towns erupted in joy. Happy people passed bottles of liquor down the street. Sacramento fired a 35 gun salute. Marysville lit a celebration fire like a big volcano in the town square. Up in the foothills, people began to look for other jobs.

Farmers and river town people rejoiced at first, but it turned out to be a hollow victory. The mine owners with heavy investments just pretended they were not washing down any "course" material and continued to blast away with water cannon to get the gold.

The problem was too big to go away. With the backing of the valley people, a business man whose office building had been flooded three times in Marysville sued the mines in Federal court. The miners felt confident that

Moonscape left by hydraulic mining with the clogged valley below. SAMCC.

These were the first environmental lawsuits in the world. Here in the Gold Country was first established the principal, still being contested every day in the 21st century, that people have a right to a healthy environment greater than the right of corporations or property owners to make a short term profit. In the end, it turned out that environment and money worked together.

It took years to stop the last desperate hydraulic miners: one of the world's first long distance telephone lines from Grass Valley to North Bloomfield was used to warn miners when the sheriff was coming. As the giant water blasting nozzles were finally shut down, the streams began to run clear again. Farmers used some of the miner's water system to begin what would become the world's largest irrigation system, slowly turning the Central Valley into the most productive farming area on the planet. Sacramento went from the capital of a gold mining district to the capital of the diverse Golden State, the richest territory in the richest country in the world.

Other Gold Mines

If miners could figure out how to contain the extra ground they washed away, they could still use water to get gold. Shoppers in Folsom drive right by Chinese Diggings, an amazing gold mine located between the Folsom Outlet Mall and the freeway at the northeast corner of the intersection of Highway 50 and Folsom Road.

Water was carefully channeled through trenches cut up to 30 feet straight down and not much wider than a person's shoulders. From the trenches the water ran though a long tunnel all the way back to the river. After the Chinese built the western railroad they were often responsible for large scale digging projects. Chinese Diggings is on the National Registry of Historic Places.

Instead of blasting away the hillside with hydraulic mining, some miners got the idea of making a huge self-propelled sluice box and created the gold-mining dredge. Normal dredges just scoop up soil and rocks under the water to make a channel deep enough for boats. A gold mining dredge scoops up sand and gravel then sorts through it looking for gold. Although there were some early attempts, gold dredging did not start along the American River until around 1900. The Sacramento area is the largest dredge field in California. There was dredging from Folsom to Carmichael, often on both sides of the river.

Gold can be found miles from water, scattered over now dry delta created millions of years ago when rivers poured out of the mountains at slightly different places. Natoma Vineyards between Rancho Cordova and Folsom once grew more grapes than Napa Valley. When they had trouble with responsible for large scale digging projects. Chinese Diggings is on the National Registry of Historic Places.

A placer mining dredge has a big arm with a conveyer belt of buckets to scoop up the gravel. This arm can be lowered or raised. Screens separate out small rocks and sand that may contain gold. Big rocks are dumped back over the side.

The gold bearing material passes over a series of riffle sluices to gold-saving tables on which mercury is sprinkled to capture the gold. When the tables are full, the gold-mercury mixture on the gold-saving tables is gathered up. The mix is taken to a treasure house and refined to separate out the gold, which was then melted and poured into gold bars.

With people and crops, land has gotten too expensive to tear up just to look for small amounts of gold. There are still treasure houses; gold mining continues in the Sacramento area as a profitable sideline to the sand and gravel business, but large scale dredging has disappeared. Estimates of the amount of gold that has been dredged around Sacramento range upwards from $1,000,000,000. Despite their profits, no law made the dredging companies restore the land, so they took the gold and left rows of exposed rock sometimes 20 feet high separated by low spots where the dredger sat.

The Rules for Mining

During the Gold Rush, when the hills became crowded with gold miners, someone had to decide who owned what. Miners were free to rip apart streams and hillsides like they would never do at home ~ there was no government. Mining towns made up their own laws and took direct action when someone broke the rules.

A miner could control a claim about as big as the floor of a small room. To keep the claim he had to work it regularly and leave his mining tools on the site to prove it. If you were the first one to discover gold in a new area, you could have a double sized claim. No slavery was allowed in the mines, even though slaves were still legal in other parts of the United States for 15 years after the Gold Rush. Far off corporations could not own claims, a miner could have other people work for him, but he had to work himself to keep his claim.

These rules may have indirectly given the world one of its great writers. A poverty stricken miner named Samuel Clemens filed what would become a multi-million dollar claim with two of his friends. Planning for riches, they all got busy out of town, each one thinking the others were doing the small amount of dig-

ging necessary to keep the claim. After ten days of no action, other miners enforced the letter of the law and legally took away the bonanza. A very disappointed young Sam Clemens got back a few minutes too late to save his claim, gave up mining and went to work writing. He became Mark Twain.

When there was crime, early miners did not take the time for long trials. Stealing was rare in the early years because when it happened, the thief was whipped and kicked out of town. Shooting and stabbing might result in the loss of an ear or branding. Murder or second offences of lesser crimes called for hanging. Placerville was first called Hangtown due to a record of administering fast justice in the town square. As one miner observed: "*When caught in the act, up they go and that's the end of it.*"

In Sacramento, citizens took the law into their own hands. After the Governor pardoned a man held by the sheriff, a vigilante committee seized the prisoner and hung him on the spot. Then

An old miner wanders out of the mountains to be amazed by the growth of Sacramento in this poster for a celebration in 1922. He should see it now. SAMCC

Stage coach robbery. Robbers could pop up anywhere and be long gone before the stage, minus some of its horses and all of its gold, hobbled into town.

they hung and burned a rag doll dressed like the Governor. When early officials were slow to punish criminals, armed citizens took over in cities all over California.

In what may have been the toughest town, Bodie, high in the mountains south of Lake Tahoe,

bad guys who shot other bad guys usually got off with a plea of self defense. But it was trouble to pick on honest citizens. The longest jail term for disorderly conduct was given to a drunk whose only crime was using "the vilest kind of language before ladies and children".

Robbers were usually polite to passengers, sometimes leaving them their money if the robbers got enough from the stage. This time it looks like they are taking up a collection. **CM, Charlie Russell.**

There were a lot of stage coach robberies. *Said one driver:*

Until you are suddenly called upon to look down the opening of a double-barreled shotgun, which has a road agent with his hand on the trigger at the other end, you have no idea how surprised you are capable of being. I have had a six-shooter pulled on me across a from table; I have proved that the hilt of a dirk (knife) can't go between two of my ribs; I have seen four aces beat a royal flush; but I was never really surprised until I looked down the muzzle of a double-barreled shotgun...

Giant gold dredges chew up the sides of rivers to find gold.
From SAMCC

Rules become Laws

To handle the Gold Rush, California needed a government. Sacramento was not the capital yet; California was not even a state, when about 50 delegates including Sutter and Vallejo got together in Monterey in the fall of 1849 to write a constitution. They had all done some prospecting, but none of them called themselves a gold miner, any more than a modern person would say he was a gambler just because he'd had been to Reno a few times.

But the laws they wrote showed they had learned a lesson about hard work and equal opportunity from the gold mines. Even though a lot of them were from states where slavery was part of every plantation, they made slavery illegal in California. Even though no other state in the Union gave women property rights, in California, from the beginning, women had the right to their own money independent of their husbands or fathers. Still far from equality, California started out ahead of other states. It took years for minorities to win the right to testify in court, even more years until women had the right to vote, but it was a start.

Expensive California

At the beginning of the Gold Rush, even ice was shipped all the way from the eastern United States. Land was cheap - people could buy a square mile of the Napa Valley for what it now costs to build a garage. Everything else was expensive. In modern money, eggs were the equivalent of $20 a dozen, butter was $30 a pound. Getting to California in 1849 could cost the equivalent of $4,000 if a passenger took 5 months to sail around South America or $10,000 to risk a two month trip across Panama. Coming overland took five months and thousands of dollars for wagons, equipment and the oxen or mules to pull them. As the Donner party found out, there was not much time to waste if you wanted to make it across. Wagon trains couldn't start until there was enough grass on the Great Plains for their animals to eat in early May and they had to make it across the Sierra Nevada mountains before the snows fell.

In Delmonico's, the best restaurant in New York, a fancy meal might cost the modern equivalent of $20. In Sacramento, a bad meal could easily be $40. Near the mines, picks and gold pans went for modern $300 each. When a shipload of cats arrived from Mexico, they sold for $200 each in modern money. California cattle were scrawny because they had been allowed to run free, rounded up for nothing but their leather hides. Eastern ranchers drove thousands of plump cows and sheep half way across America to feed the gold miners. Early farmers sold watermelons to miners for modern $40 each. Lots of Califomians had the money to pay these high prices: in 1852, gold made a billion and a half dollars in modern money.

Sacramento and Troy

Heinrich Schliemann was a kind of real life Indiana Jones. He eventually uncovered the site of Troy and found many ancient treasures. Before that, he made the first part of the fortune he needed to pay for his adventures as a gold dealer in Sacramento. Afraid of fire, he got an office in the only brick building in town near the river on J Street. Afraid of thieves, he slept on top of his gold with a pistol in each hand. In one year in Sacramento he made millions of dollars in modern money. This Gold Country treasure funded even more business success when he returned to Europe and allowed him to be the first person to uncover much of the ancient Greek world. While he was digging for historic artifacts, the ones he liked best were those made out of gold.

Never Say Die

In its first five years, Sacramento lived through five floods, four fires and the shooting of both the mayor and the sheriff in the Squatter's Riot (see Golden Voices, Chapter 7). A cholera epidemic killed 1 out of 10 people in less than a month; you could go from healthy to dead in one day. Many people left town, but the doctors bravely stayed with their patients even though they had a 1 in 3 chance of dying themselves. In the early years as many as 20% of all gold seekers died during their first year in California. Said one pioneer:

Our drinking water is living - that is it is composed of one third green fine moss, one third pollywogs, and one third embryo mosquitoes... these we strain through our teeth.

Fires burned down the stores of three of the four Sacramento shopkeepers who would later build the transcontinental railroad. Only Leland Stanford's grocery was still standing. Huntington, Crocker and Hopkins could have given up, but instead they joined the rest of Sacramento to rebuild their town as soon as the flames died away.

After a two month flood in the early 1860's, newspapers in other towns said Sacramento was doomed. Unwilling to float away, the citizens paid for thousands of wagon loads of rocks and soil to actually raise downtown buildings and streets a full story above flood waters. There are still houses in downtown Sacramento with the main entrance on the second story to be ready for floods. Many downtown streets are hollow, with the old first story of Gold Rush buildings buried under them. People did what they could to survive.

At the center of the Gold Rush, Sacramento never gave up.

Some of the ancient gold from Troy that Schliemann, the real life Indiana Jones, discovered using the money he made trading California gold in Sacramento.

Chapter Seven

Voices From Gold Country

They were rough in those times! They fairly reveled in gold, whisky, fights and fandangos, and they were unspeakably happy. . .
Mark Twain in Roughing It

Between the time of the Indians and the cities, there were lots of people with good stories to tell. By listening to their real voices, we can understand what it felt like.

Indians

The Indians liked games and gambling:

Sometimes a football game was called, the women playing the men, putting up valuables and even money to bet with each other. The men kicked the ball with the foot while the women caught it with the hand and ran with it. The men hugged the woman who carried the ball. When they tickled her belly, she threw the ball to another woman…that was their playing together so a man could hug the woman he loved. The women on their part took every opportunity to hug the men they

loved; the game was like that so that this could be done.
William Joseph, Nisenan

The first non-Indians to camp here, Jedediah Smith and his men are surrounded by Nisenan near the American River in 1827:

I endeavored to convince them of my disposition to be friendly by every means in my power but to no purpose. They considered all my friendly signs caused by my own weakness. Of our guns they had never seen the effects and supposed them solid sticks which we could only use in close contest. Whatever may have been their views, they pressed so closely and in such numbers on my party that I was obliged to look for an advantageous piece of ground on which to make a stand against the threatening danger. Having found a favorable position I again tried to convince them of my friendly disposition but to no purpose. Their preparations were still going forward and their parties were occupying favorable points around me. Seeing what must be the inevitable consequence I determined to anticipate them in the commencement and wishing to them as little harm as possible and yet consistent with my own safety, I ordered 2 men to fire (of course not the most uncertain marksmen.) I preferred long shots that it might give them the idea that we could kill at any distance. At the report of the guns, both men firing at once, two Indians fell.

*F*or a moment the Indians stood still and silent as if a thunderbolt had fallen among them. Then a few words passed from party to party and in a moment they ran like deer.

Jedediah Smith, 1827

State of the art equipment and quality tools were forged near the mines. **Photo: Tom Meyers.**

The Indians had a different idea of fighting:

Battles between tribes or fights between individuals were never intended to purposely kill people, Grandpa stressed. Advance and retreat, tease and taunt, humiliate the enemy, he counseled. Killing was seldom necessary. Rather, he said, to touch one's enemy, to play with him and shame him, was to gain honor and esteem from one's peers. If you have to fight, he said, do so only in this way.

Gaylen Lee, Mono

The Indians felt they had an understanding with some animals:

You know, daughter, before the Spaniards came to California, the bears and us used to gather berries together. The bears were real friendly. We got along real well. We could talk to each other, and we had a good understanding. When the Spaniards came, they found it pretty easy to shoot the bears. After that the bears wouldn't go berrying with us anymore.

Semu Huaute, Chumash

Mexicans

Under Mexican rule, Mariano Vallejo owned a huge ranch and was the most important person in California. Friend to Indians and settlers, he was arrested during the American takeover and held prisoner, to Sutter's great embarrassment, at Sutter's Fort.

In the takeover, he lost almost everything:

What misery!...This country was the true Eden, the land of promise where hunger was never known.
[Later, to his family] Believe me, Ricardo, American democracy is the best democracy in the world No, let it go... Let the wound heal.

General Mariano Vallejo

Entertainment

Opening night at the first theatre built in California; the canvas walled Eagle Theater on the waterfront in Old Sacramento. The play is The Bandit Chief; or the Spectre of the Forest

Several acts are filled with the usual amount of fighting and terrible speeches; but the interest of the play is carried to an awful height by the appearance of two

Slowly, farming took over from gold mining as the biggest money maker in the Sacramento area. **From: SM, Bianchi.**

spectres (ghosts), clad in mutilated tent-covers, and holding spermaceti candles in their hands. At this juncture Mrs. Ray rushes in and throws her self into an attitude in the middle of the stage: why she does it, no one can tell. This movement, which she repeats several times in the course of the first three acts, has no connection with the tragedy; it is evidently introduced for the purpose of showing the audience that there is, actually, a female performer. The miners, to whom the sight of a woman is not a frequent occurrence, are delighted with these passages and applaud vehemently.

Bayard Taylor, 1849

Pioneers

The young Swiss merchant de Rutte travels up the Sacramento River with John Sutter in 1850.

They see a wild looking man in a canoe; Sutter goes to sit in the canoe and talk to the man who de Rutte watches:

His lively expression was pierced by a look which, when by chance he turned my way, seemed to take me in from top to bottom. His clothes, as I have said, were in tatters. He was wearing a red shirt with tears in the sleeves and at the elbows, black pants, gaping at the knees and fringed at the cuffs, which flapped at his tall miner's boots. Either this man suffered from abject poverty or else he had just survived a battle with men, beasts or nature! After a quarter of an hour, the captain (Sutter) once again shook his hand and returned to our boat. The stranger seized his paddle and disappeared around the bend.

Without waiting for our questions Captain Sutter assuaged our curiosity and said: "I wager, my friends, that you will never guess who that man is with whom I have just spoken, and yet as threadbare as he is, history will record his name next to mine—and I will add that a century from now, possibly Captain Sutter will be forgotten, while the American will have conserved in his annals the name of this man who is an American citizen. Yes, this voyager is none other than James Marshall, the very man who discovered gold while building my mill. Just as you have seen him, he wanders from mountain to mountain and from gully to gully, looking for new mines which he abandons to others as soon as they are discovered... It is his mania, you might even say his folly...

Theophile de Rutte, 1850

90

Sam Brannan, master promoter, writing in the *California Star,* 1848:

Gold deposits can be found at random and dug without trouble.

Sam Brannan was serving as judge and John Sutter was on the jury of a murder trial in Sacramento. Contrary to all legal rules, Brannan and Sutter were passing a bottle of brandy back and forth as the trial went on. Brannan, perhaps forgetting he was the judge, leaped up and started to make an argument supporting the prosecution.

The defendant objected: *"Hold on Brannan! You're the judge."*
"I know it", said Brannan, *"and I'm the prosecuting attorney too!"*

Later, Sutter was offended when the defense said bad things about the dead man, who had been a friend of Sutter's:

"Gentlemen", said Sutter, *"the man is dead and has atoned for his faults, and I will not sit here and hear his character traduced."*

With that, Sutter grabbed the brandy bottle and headed for the door. Caring more about the booze then the trial, Brannan begged him to come back. The defendant was eventually acquitted.

Traveling merchant de Rutte on the site of the first big gold strike, just up stream from what would become Folsom:

At the time I visited Mormon Island, the gravel of this islet must have already been turned over more than fifty or even a hundred times, but it possessed that fabulous advantage that each time the waters rose and submerged it, they deposited with each ebb a new layer of gold-bearing sand. The richness of this little island seemed inexhaustible and even a miner modest enough to content himself with a daily take of five to six dollars ($100 in modern money) was sure to find there an honest remuneration for his labor... it was here the poor miner, coming from San Francisco, stopped and tried to make enough money to continue on his way to the higher and more favorable country.
Theophile de Rutte, 1850

A small army of settlers fought the government over land rights in the Squatter's Riot of 1850. Hit by a bullet, the Mayor of Sacramento falls backwards.

Across the street, one of the squatters has been shot. Reenacted near where it happened in Old Sacramento. **Photo: Noel Neuburger.**

Squatters or Settlers

New settlers arriving after months of hard travel could not believe the mostly empty land in downtown Sacramento was already taken. Settlers did not see anybody living on the land and the absentee owners said they bought it from John Sutter, whose own claim to be able to sell the land came from a Mexican grant. The United States had just beaten Mexico in a war. Some new arrivals grabbed unused land and built temporary shelters, thus becoming squatters. When the courts ordered them off, forty of them marched with guns to 4th and J Streets.

The Mayor of Sacramento ordered them to stop. They shot him. In the gun battle that followed, the leader of the squatters died but others escaped. The next night the Sheriff led a charge into a bar in the country where the squatters were hiding. He was shot dead at the door. His deputies burst into the room and talked the owner of the bar who was aiming at them from a balcony upstairs into laying down his shotgun. Then they wheeled around in fright as squatters hiding behind the bar popped up and began to shoot. In an almost blind face to face gun fight in a dark and smoky barroom, some deputies got shot but they arrested most of the squatters.

Even citizens who had sympathized with the squatters now knew they had to enforce the law. Armed volunteers helped the government patrol the streets. Still, there was mercy: the surviving squatters were pardoned and one even got elected to the legislature while he was in jail. But, after this Squatter's Riot of 1850, most people respected the orders of the government, even if they worked to change them.

One squatter did not. The posse brought Henry Caulfield to jail tied backwards on his horse, but he was released. Caulfield shot at a judge in a courtroom a year later and missed with all his bullets. The judge was about to kill Henry when a policeman saved his life. Four years later, Caulfield was shot several times outside the Read building. As he lay near death a priest said "I am told you are a very bad man". Caulfield yelled, "It's a damn lie ... and you're no doctor. Get the hell out of here." Caulfield recovered.

The riverboat Daisy chugging all the way through Sacramento up the American River to Folsom during extreme high water. Don't try this today. In the inset close-up, note the cargo of logs and the non-stop party on deck.
Great Wall by Hugh Gorman.

A year later, Caulfield was losing a fight on the second floor of a house when he fell out the window. His opponent turned himself in to the sheriff, but by the time they got there to pick up the body, Caulfield had somehow come to and crawled to the hospital. He lived behind the Crocker Art Gallery and he used to insult Judge Crocker, who ignored him. Caulfield spent six years in San Quentin in the 1880's for killing a man. All told he was in more than 20 deadly fights over almost 40 year and survived them all. He was walking peacefully down the tracks on R Street near his home when somehow he did not notice the evening train from Folsom roaring into town. He drank a lot. Caulfield the trouble making survivor was killed because he did not see the one thing most people could not miss, a speeding train.

A New Dawn

The American River generated the first hydroelectric power ever transmitted long distance (22 miles from Folsom). This made Sacramento the first city in the world lit by the power of a river. The city celebrated with a Carnival of Lights in 1895.

Here is the *Sacramento Bee's* glowing account:

The lightning blazed and flooded Sacramento's streets with lakes of liquid fire. A glorious dawning; then glowed the sunlight of an aurora of progress and prosperity. A dazzling tableau of moving lights, beautiful girls, and fairy-like pavilions, made a spectacle unequaled for brilliancy and splendor in the annals of electricity. The trees in front of the Capitol glowed with incandescent lamps.

There was a 150 foot high may pole of lights which shown like a pillar of fire in the plaza in front of City Hall. Thousands of people came from San Francisco to see. The parade went on till after midnight. A 24,000 candle power arc light on top of the Capitol dome could be seen 100 miles away in the foothills. A speaker said:

Sacramento... cast aside the old and fabled robes of her humble childhood days and stood at the altar of celestial fire to be made the bride of Progress of the new century that is about to dawn.

Sacramento lit up with water power electricity from its own American River only 30 years after the Civil War. The glow from the Carnival of Lights could be seen from the hills of Gold Country.

*The day after the Mayor was shot; the Sheriff rode out to arrest the squatters.
He was killed, but in a wild face to face gun fight in a dark and smokey barroom,
his deputies arrested most of the squatters. Reenacted.* **Photo: Noel Neuburger.**

Chapter Eight
GETTING AROUND

**When business is lively and three or four steamers
and twice as many other vessels are unloading every day,
the levee is a tangled mass of men and rogues and Mexicans
and Chinese and Chileans and Kanakas [Hawaiians]
and horses and mules and asses and oxen...
and pickles and oysters and yams and cabbages and books
and furniture and almost everything one could think of--
except honesty and religion.**
Israel Lord on Sacramento, 1850

Even before cars and planes, people traveled as fast as they could go. The Pony Express galloped, riverboats raced and travelers let their butts get bumped around for 30 hours straight to make fast stagecoach time. Sacramento was the hub of a golden wheel of transportation.

For Indians, miners, and settlers, the rivers were the easiest way to travel. Even today, the railroad and 1-80 to Reno partly parallel the North Fork of the American while Highway 50 to South Lake Tahoe goes in the direction of the South Fork of the River. Riverboats ran up and down the Sacramento River several times a day; the fastest took about six hours to get to San Francisco. A few times brave riverboats even made it up the American River to Folsom during high water. One ended up stuck in an orchard in Sacramento after squirting through a break in the levee.

The earliest travel routes along the banks of the rivers were Nisenan Indian trails. Sutter's workmen and early gold miners followed an Indian route along the American River to reach the sawmill site at Coloma. Most important California routes are not new: underneath the smooth pavement is usually a dirt wagon road used for a hundred years, underneath that an Indian trail walked on by bare feet for a thousand years and below that a path that guided animals for tens of thousands of years. Like water running downhill, travelers found a natural guide to them.

Crossing the Rivers

Before bridges, ferries made good money giving rides across the river in boats pulled along a rope hand-over-hand. The fees for the ferry service were $30 in modern money for a person on foot, $80 for a rider and horse during the day, or $160 at night.

Captain Childs lived across the river from Sacramento with his three young daughters. Since there were about 19 men for every woman during the early days, Captain Child's daughters were very popular. Young men who showed up to visit after dark and were too proud to leave their horses behind ended up paying modern $320 roundtrip. It is not recorded whether anybody found true love, but the ferryman was happy.

By 1855 there were at least five ferries in operation across the American in Sacramento and the prices begin to go down. Then bridges begin to go up, at first toll bridges built by money making individuals and eventually free bridges built by the government. Toll or free, at least one bridge seemed to wash away every year in the winter floods.

Supplies

When the State of California failed to come up with money for a road across the Sierra, Sacramento went into partnership with Placer and Yolo counties. They built a road from Placerville to Lake Tahoe 12 feet wide, cleared of brush and rocks, along the south fork of the American River pretty much where Highway 50 goes today. In a stroke of fortune, it opened just in time for the discovery of silver in Nevada.

Traffic jams are nothing new. There were sometimes so many people on the road that it was difficult for wagons to get on. Early traffic jams could limit progress to a few miles a day. The first big success of the Central Pacific Railroad was not a railroad at all, but a dirt highway they built where the railroad was going to go. That provided a road through Auburn near where Freeway 80 goes today. Wagon drivers who had to get up to the mountains loved the Auburn road; the tolls they paid provided badly needed cash to build the railroad.

Clipper ships were the fastest sailors in the world. Excited gold seekers packed on so tight they even sat in the lifeboats, talking about the wonders of their Gold Country destination as the ship knifed through the waves.
The quickest voyage ever made was piloted by a woman. **Colonized CSL**

Years before at the beginning of the Gold Rush, wagons for carrying supplies got stuck on narrow trails once they reached the edge of town. Even after the main roads were built to Auburn and Placerville, there were still hundreds of mining towns that only mules could reach. Fortunately, mules are tough and each one could carry 300 pounds almost anywhere. Thousands of mules walked the steep mountain trails covering an average of 30 miles a day and carrying everything from whiskey to pianos. They used a soft straw-stuffed leather pack saddle that the Mexicans invented. It was a big improvement for the animals over the wooden saddles the Americans used and soon the U.S. Army went to the Mexican system.

At first, freight was hauled on recycled emigrant wagons brought down from Oregon after crossing the plains. They could not move enough. Mechanics built their own California wagons, some of which could carry up to 15 tons. With a trailer, big wagons could haul as much as a modern truck. Since every miner needed at least a pound of goods a day, moving supplies was a major business. Hundreds of teams left Sacramento for the mines every day. In 1852 some 137,000 tons of goods worth $160,000,000 today were shipped out of Sacramento. In 1856, a traveler passed 82 teams, all heavily loaded, between Sacramento and Placerville—an average of one every half mile.

Sometimes the dust was so thick that it filled the air for 20 feet above the ground, like a choking brown fog. When it rained, oxen, horses and people could sink into the mud above their legs. Some people even set out bundles of hay for their half buried horses to eat while they waited for teams with a rope to pull them out.

Stage Coaches

The early 49ers with enough money could get a ride on a stage coach between Sacramento and the gold fields. James Birch arrived in Sacramento from Rhode Island in the summer of 1849 with a coach for his own stage line. His first route began at Sacramento and soon extended to Coloma. A few months before, the 50-mile road that the stage followed had been a narrow walk-it-yourself pack trail following the American River up into the mountains. When it was the only stage in California, tickets prices were sky high: more than it would cost to fly to Europe in modern money.

of eight coaches and 100 horses. Coach companies carried gold from the mines as well as passengers. Sixteen or more people could be crammed into and on top of a wooden coach that was the size that an SUV is today.

An old wagon in modern Placerville. **Photo: Tom Meyers.**

Only a year after Birch started, there were several lines running regularly out of Sacramento. Prices went down and riders went up. In two more years there were 12 different companies, each with an average

Stage coaches got their name because they often operated in stages of about 100 miles a day, usually stopping at night so their cramped occupants could stretch out and spend the night in some kind of bed. But not always: the run from Sacramento to Shasta was straight through—30 hours of bouncing over 188 miles of potholes and rocks. Stage drivers made few attempts to avoid bumps, choosing instead to let the horses pick their way down the road so the team could find their way at night or in fog.

Brave Charlie

Charlie Parkhurst drove a Well Fargo stage for almost 20 years. Surprised by a stage robber, Charlie didn't have a gun and was forced to give up a treasure box full of gold. When it happened a second time, Charlie whipped out a shotgun, whirled around and blasted the robber in the chest. Bringing an overloaded stage down a tough mountain track, handing a team of horses with command and respect, having a couple of whiskeys after a run, Charlie was known as one of the best of the boys. Except, after Charlie died, it turned out Charlie was a woman. She had escaped an orphanage years ago dressed as a boy and just kept it that way. Dressed like a man, she was the first woman to vote in the United States.

Rattlesnake Dick

When he started out, Dick Barter was not a bad guy. He tried so hard to find gold at Rattlesnake Bar, near what is now the top of Folsom Lake, that folks started calling him Rattlesnake Dick. Maybe because of his non-stop energy, twice he was falsely accused of stealing someone else's animals. Although he was eventually found innocent both times, even after years the stories still followed him. Finally he decided he might as well live up to his bad reputation. He robbed a man of valuables worth $8,000 in modern money and told him to let everybody know he had been held up by Rattlesnake Dick.

Rattlesnake Dick and his gang held up stages and even a whole mule train loaded with gold before he finally died in a shootout with the sheriff. A glittering horde of Dick's stolen gold is still hidden somewhere in the hills.

Wells Fargo

Wells Fargo used stages and delivery services to move mail,

Stage coach robbery.
CMagazine, Wyeth.

gold and supplies all over the west. You can still see their first office in Old Sacramento. Wells Fargo had branches all over the gold country by the late 1850s where people picked up mail, deposited gold and money, and shipped packages. Today's Wells Fargo Bank is a direct descendent of those early services that began in Sacramento and San Francisco.

There were hundreds of stage robberies and stage robbers were rarely caught. Stagecoaches peaked during the years before the railroads. Even though trains took over the main lines, stages still covered all the towns off the train lines from railway terminals such as Folsom, Auburn, Lincoln and Newcastle until automobiles arrived. Wells Fargo does not run stages anymore, but it remains one of the largest banks. Some bus companies still run that are descended from stage lines.

Getting the Mail Through

There was no mail delivery to the 49ers at the mines. If you wanted to get a letter in the early days, you had to stand in line for hours at the post office in San Francisco. By the end of 1849, enterprising private delivery services were available to help, for a price. It cost a dollar for the delivery service to check to see if you had a letter in San Francisco or Sacramento and a full ounce of gold if they actually found one to bring to you. That brought the cost of receiving a letter at the mines to more than $300 in modern money; well worth it to a miner who often hadn't seen his family for a year or more.

By the 1850s there were over 60 delivery services, each covering a small area of high mountain valleys. When the snows got too heavy for horses, the deliverymen ploughed ahead on foot. They were inspired by John Snowshoe.

Thompson who brought the first skis to the Sierra from his native Norway. For 20 years, no matter how bad the storm, Snowshoe Thompson always made it across the mountains, climbing up one side and skiing down the other.

Pony Express

The Pony Express moved mail by non-stop horse relays across

the west between Sacramento and Missouri in 10 days. Running in 1860 and 1861, the Pony Express charged what would be $50 in modern money to deliver a letter.

Most riders were around 20; the youngest was 11 and the oldest was about 45. They were not very big, usually weighing around 120 pounds. The Pony Express ran day and night, summer and winter. Taking off at a gallop, as fast as their horse would go, riders left from both Sacramento and Missouri twice a week. The place where the Pony Express route began is marked by a statue on Second Street in Old Sacramento, the route went through Placerville. There were stations every 10 or 15 miles where riders got a fresh horse; new riders took over every hundred miles or so. The route was 2,000 miles of full speed riding.

The Pony Express kept communications opened to California at the beginning of the Civil War and proved that determined men could move across the country even in winter. This helped give people courage to build the railroad. The Pony Express shut down with the coming of the overland telegraph in 1861,

explaining that, although they were fast, they could not compete with lightning.

Good Roads

Except for privately built and operated toll highways, roads were a local responsibility. The key Folsom Road was declared a public highway by the Sacramento County Board of Supervisors in 1859, four years after the railroad took over most of the Folsom bound freight.

Even before there were cars, political pressures to improve the roads in California begin to build. Farmers, bicycle clubs and store owners got together for a Goods Roads Convention and statewide demand finally resulted in the Bureau of Highways, the grandfather of CalTrans. The State's first report was the proposal for the road that is now Highway 50, bringing up to date the dirt road Sacramento area counties had bravely built themselves 30 years before.

As more people began to have automobiles, a macadam hard surface was put over the dusty

Steam locomotive near the Railroad Museum. **Photo: Tom Meyers.**

main streets and new bridges were built. Until the Yolo Causeway was opened in 1916, it took six hours of zigzagging through the muddy tule marsh to drive to San Francisco - in good weather. In the winter, the road could be flooded out for months. That is why riverboats stayed popular. Even a drive from Carmichael to downtown and back could take most of the day.

Bridges

Being surrounded by water, the Sacramento area has to be surrounded by bridges. With the beginning of the 1900's, new bridges crossed the American River to support the development of suburban Sacramento, Carmichael and Fair Oaks.

At Folsom a wire suspension bridge was constructed in 1857. This wire bridge looked nice, but it was destroyed by a flood after only five years. More bridges were built culminating in the amazing steel truss bridge that first spanned the 300 foot canyon in 1893. Said to be the finest bridge in California when it was built, it carried horses, cattle, early bicycles and cars across the American River until the job was taken over by the present concrete Rainbow Bridge in 1917.

For years, the 1893 steel bridge stood unused as traffic poured over the newer Rainbow Bridge a few feet away. Finally in 1931, since it was so sturdy, the little bridge was carefully taken apart and moved 200 miles to span the Klamath River in far northern California. More than 100 years after it was originally built, it was no longer needed on the Klamath, but Folsom wanted a bicycle bridge. That is when the steel span became The Little Bridge That Came Home. It was painstakingly taken apart by workers whose great grandfathers probably were not even born when the bridge was first built. They moved it back to Folsom and set it carefully on the same piers on which it stood 100 years before. Of course it fit perfectly. You can bicycle across it just upstream from the Rainbow Bridge.

The next bridge downstream is the Hazel Avenue Bridge, built by Sacramento County in 1966. Although it is a highway bridge, there is a special passage for bicycles and horses connecting the trail along the American River Parkway. People who

bicycle under, instead of over the Hazel Bridge, find a trail that connects the Fish Hatchery with Old Folsom along the south side of the river.

As the old village of Fair Oaks grew up in the early 1900's, a bridge was built to connect the town to a railroad stop across the river. This bridge is closed to traffic but opened to bikes, pedestrians and horses. In 2001 it got a new plastic composite deck. The Old Fair Oaks Bridge is the scene of a local howling at the moon tradition on clear full moon nights, started by area artists in the 1960's. Above the northeastern end of the bridge are the beautiful Fair Oaks Bluffs.

Car bridges and bike bridges cross the American River. The Jibboom Street Bridge, near the mouth of the American River, links Sacramento City with the Garden Highway. This drawbridge— the only one on the American River-- was built in 1929 when people were still not quite ready to admit that the American River is too shallow for ships. Jibboom Street was named for the forest of jibs and booms of the Gold Rush sailing ships that used to dock near it. Now the old bridge carries bicyclists

Sacramento bicycle club on an excursion. Most of the bikes are speedy and dangerous high wheelers. The bike in the middle marks the beginning of modern bikes with equal sized wheels. Called "safety bikes" then, they were originally looked down upon as too slow.
Colorized. CSL

to Old Sacramento and cars to Discovery Park where the clear American River joins the muddy Sacramento.

The No Hands Bridge

outside of Auburn carries bicycles, horses and people. When it was built it was the longest concrete arch bridge in the world. It has stood for almost 100 years while more modern bridges have been washed away by floods.

It is called No Hands because until recently the 150 foot high

American River on high wheel bicycles more than 100 years ago.

Since the roads were too crowded and muddy for good riding, the Wheelmen taxed themselves the modern equivalent of $20 each to build a gravel bicycle path to Folsom. When the first section opened, hundreds of bicyclists, women in their long skirts and men in knickers, rode out happily on their bikes. The private bike path builders ran out of money by the time they got out to what is now Hazel Avenue, so Folsom businesspeople came up with the cash to finish the path.

The record speed a hundred years ago from Old Sacramento to Folsom was just over an hour. Today a racer can ride the 20 mile bike trail from Sacramento to Folsom in 50 minutes, just 10 minutes faster then the clip set by their gutsy great-great grandfathers. And modern riders are spinning on pavement, with bikes weighing half as much as the one speed clunkers from the 1800's.

Bicyclists in 1900 rode partly because they didn't have cars. Bicycles were the first chance a lot of people had to get around;

bridge had no guardrails, a test of nerves for riders or runners.

Bike Path

Roads are for fun as well as for getting places. The Capital City Wheelmen raced along the horses cost too much for most people to keep. With the arrival of the affordable automobile, the idea of a bike trail got lost for about 60 years. Public support helped create the modern 33 mile Jedediah Smith Memorial Bicycle Trail beginning in the 1960's. The trail was finished in 1985 all the way from Old Sacramento to Beal's Point, miles past Folsom on Folsom Lake.

River Boats

It could take most of a week to sail and row from San Francisco to Sacramento before the Gold Rush - the crew of the small boats that dropped off John Sutter almost starved in the days it took them to get back home.

It was like the difference between walking and driving when the first steamboat, the Senator, chugged into the Sacramento wharf after spending most of 1849 fighting its way around South America from Boston.

Said one Sacramento citizen:
All the nymphs of the ocean making their appearance in our midst would not have excited more rejoicing and excitement than this noble floating palace...

Suddenly, San Francisco was less than a day away from the gold mines. Business was amazing. One way tickets costing the equivalent of $600 in modern money sold out every day. The side-wheeler Senator took in almost $40,000,000 in modern money in one year. It made more than the biggest gold mine in California that year, proving once again that mining miners was almost always better than mining mines.

That kind of money attracted lots of other competing boats and within a few years fares dropped from modern $600 to $20.00. To attract attention, steamboats raced each other to Sacramento. At least five of them exploded when they tried to pump too much steam into their early boilers. More than 100 people were killed in river boat explosions and another 10 drowned when one riverboat rammed another racing toward gold country. Sometimes the crews even shot at each other.

When they were not being blown up, passengers enjoyed the races. Riverboats had the best food, drink, dancing and gambling around. Even when laws

Steamboats and shipping office in Old Sacramento.
Photo: Tom Meyers.

were passed against wild living in the first part of the 1900's, paddle wheelers acted as if there were no rules on the river. The twin boats Delta King and Delta Queen are still around: the King is a floating hotel and restaurant in Old Sacramento and the Queen cruises the Mississippi River.

Railroads

In the early days, people dreamed of railroads. There were no cars and no paved highways. Depending on the weather, the dirt roads were often clogged with either mud or dust. Stages made up for being slow by being uncomfortable. Riverboats only worked on the Sacramento; a few brave captains made it up to Folsom on the American River during high water, only to end up stuck in low water.

The west's first railroad was originally planned to link Sacramento with Negro Bar and Marysville, two of the most important mining distribution centers in the state. The railroad's designer was Theodore Judah, the young visionary who would later design the transcontinental railroad. When the Sacramento Valley Railroad ran out of money, they had to settle for just reaching Negro Bar, which became Folsom.

The west's first train locomotive, the Sacramento, arrived from Boston lashed to the deck of a ship that had sailed around the bottom of South America. The railroad was still feverishly laying tracks, so the day after the engine arrived they took 200 cheering guests as far as they could go—all the way from Old Sacramento to 17th Street. A few weeks later an excited Judah made a gold ring from ore workers found while cutting through a bluff of the river to build tracks.

By early 1856 the tracks were finished to Folsom, the new town just above Negro Bar that Judah had surveyed. A gala celebration opened the railroad with special trains to Folsom, where over one thousand people danced all night long at the Railroad Ball.

The initial schedule had two trains running from Sacramento and two from Folsom every day. It cost a passenger $40 in modern money. Supplies went up to the mountains and gold came down:

The cars (of the railroad) came in to connect with the up-country stages every morning at a quarter before eight... As soon as the cars reached the platform, (a Wells Fargo guard) handed out the treasure, put up in bags marked with the names of the different stages and locked all the safes... It was a close shave sometimes. I have had melted gold in the fire when the five minute bell rang, poured in, dressed the bar, chipped it, weighed, sealed and way billed it, and had it on the cars in time.

(Charles Blake, 1861)

In 1861, the new Central California Railroad hooked up with the Sacramento Valley Railroad at Folsom and ran trains as far as Lincoln. The Central California had been trying to get to Marysville but ran out of money after building a huge bridge across the American River canyon. The bridge was located near the present Rainbow Bridge over the river at Folsom. Modern-day Greenback Lane follows the railroad right-of-way north of the river.

The railroad bridge lasted until 1867 when it collapsed into the river with a thunderous roar. By that time the California Central from Folsom to Roseville had been abandoned because the Central Pacific Railroad direct from Sacramento was a much easier way to get to Roseville.

Gold Country Railroads

A number of short railroads went to towns and mines in the Sierra foothills. The Sacramento, Placer and Nevada Railroad started out with big plans but its name turned out to be almost longer than its tracks which only made it from Folsom most of the way to Auburn along what is now Auburn Folsom Road. The S, P and N station now in Old Folsom is the oldest still standing railroad station in the west.

The Nevada County Narrow Gauge Railroad squeezed through the mountains on smaller tracks from Colfax to Nevada City. People called the NCNG "never come, never go" because it was often late. In 1893, a circus train on this usually safe railroad jumped the tracks with lots of people and animals hurt.

Central Pacific

Gold was discovered on the

THE RIV

SAN FRANCISCO
LEAVE 6.30 P.M.

It took half a day by riverboat from San Francisco to Sacramento. Early roads were bad and even if you rode the train, you still had to take a boat across the Bay. It was easy to justtify an overnight river cruise and beside, there was usually a party on board.
SAMCC

ER LINES

ily SACRAMENTO

ARRIVE 5.30 A.M.

American River at almost the exact time Mexico officially gave up the territory to the Americans. As soon as the word got out, people realized they needed a railroad to connect the rest of the country with its newly valuable state.

The big money was in New York and San Francisco, so it is somewhat surprising that the men who finally organized the transcontinental railroad were small time shop keepers in Sacramento. Mark Hopkins and Collis Huntington had a hardware store, Leland Stanford was a grocer and Charles Crocker sold clothes and sewing supplies. They were ordinary people selling ordinary things; the total value of everything they owned was about $100,000— even in today's money none of them was a millionaire.

Theodore Judah, the company's visionary chief engineer, had even less money, but he was rich in ideas. Judah had designed the short railroad from Sacramento to Folsom five years before.

Now he planned to parallel the north fork of the American River then go over the Sierra Nevada all the way back East. He didn't live to see the railroad finished, but almost 150 years later; trains still roll on the route he laid out. There is a monument to him at 2nd and L streets in Old Sacramento.

The Big Four, Crocker, Hopkins, Huntington and Stanford, may not have been rich, but they were all Republicans. At one time they were almost the only members in Sacramento of that new anti-slavery party that sprung up in the Gold Rush years before the Civil War. The Big Four decided to try to build a railroad within days of learning that Abraham Lincoln had been elected as the first Republican president. A few months later they held their first organizational meeting within days of learning that the Confederates had fired the first shots that started the Civil War.

Stanford had run for office twice in years past and been defeated. In the passionate heat of the first days of the Civil War, five months after the railroad company was organized, he was elected Governor of California.

The Central Pacific Railroad started building from the docks in Sacramento in 1863 and finally joined the Union Pacific coming from the East in 1869 in the middle of Utah. It almost did not happen. Even with Leland Stanford as Governor, no one wanted to invest in the railroad. The Big Four were ready to give up when Collis Huntington made a desperate trip to see the Ames Shovel Company back East. Huntington's hardware store had sold a lot of shovels and always paid Ames on time. The Ames brothers agreed to a loan if Huntington would personally guarantee it with every cent he owned or ever hoped to earn. Frightened to the bottom of his thrifty soul, Huntington agreed.

Meanwhile, Governor of California and President of the railroad Stanford had pushed through legislation to get funding from both the state and the Sacramento area to start construction. The move got blocked in court, so Stanford appointed Edwin Crocker as Chief Justice of the Supreme Court. This move set a record for conflict of interest: Edwin was the chief lawyer of the railroad and the brother of railroad owner Charles Crocker. Without batting an eye, Edwin Crocker dismissed the legal challenges and the difficult job of building the longest railroad in the world began.

Building a bridge across the American River and other early construction was so expensive that Charles Crocker said:

I would have been glad, when we had thirty miles of road built, to have got a clean shirt... I owed everybody that would trust me, and would have been glad for them to forgive my debts and take everything I had, even the furniture of my family, and to have gone into the world and started anew.

The Central Pacific was not only the longest railroad ever attempted, but also the first one to cross a mountain range like the Sierra Nevada. One snow storm screamed and blew for two weeks straight and that was just one of 44 snowstorms in the winter the railroad pushed over the mountains. An avalanche carried away 20 Chinese workers. Even the biggest snowplow pushed by ten locomotives could not clear the track. Using picks and shovels, 2,000 desperate workers attacked the icy drifts, fighting to open a 15 mile path for life giving supplies to the thousands of Chinese

Train wrecks did not happen that often, but they scared people the way plane crashes do today. The circus train went off the tracks near Nevada City.
From CSL.

workers blasting tunnels through the mountainside. Ox carts tried to struggle through the snow, but the drifts began to bury them. Frantic drivers twisted the tails of oxen to make them go. The bellowing animals would sink down, struggle forward a few hundred feet, and then sink again. Some of the animals had to be abandoned, their tails twisted off.

Working as Huntington said: "as though Heaven was before you and Hell was behind you", tunnels, bridges and 40 miles of snow sheds to protect the tracks eventually led the Central Pacific down from the mountains. The western railroad met up in Utah with the Southern Pacific Railroad which had been building across relatively easy flat land from the east. It was the miracle of the age and, like the Gold Rush, it started in Sacramento.

Great Train Robberies

The people responsible for shipping gold at Wells Fargo

were relieved that they could send treasure over the mountains on what they thought were safe trains instead of on easy to rob stage coaches. Surprise: robbers jumped on a slow moving train on its way down from Lake Tahoe to Reno; forced the guards to open the safe and hit the trail with gold worth in modern money more than $800,000. They didn't bother to take the silver because it was too heavy. Only a year after the railroad got started, this was the first train robbery on the west coast.

T he robbers were clever, except for the little detail of getting away. The authorities immediately offered a reward as big as the treasure that was stolen. One of the robbers wore gambler's boots which left a high heeled track in the snow. Three of them checked into a lonely country inn a few miles from the robbery. They pretended that they did not know each other but spent so much time talking that the landlady got suspicious. An intrepid Nevada sheriff followed the dumb robbers into California and arrested two of them in their sleep. After these guys were "sweated" in separate questioning, they soon

spilled the beans on the rest of the crew.

The leader of the robber gang turned out to be a respected businessman and Sunday school teacher in the boomtown of Virginia City. When the sheriff came to see him, the businessman coolly said he thought the law men didn't have any idea who did the robbery. The sheriff said, "Oh yes we do. It's you." The businessman-robber turned blue.

The robbers were convicted and most of the gold was recovered. But treasure hunters still search for 150 gold coins, each one now worth almost $500, buried somewhere along the Truckee River between Reno and California. That's not all. After the train was robbed near the California-Nevada boarder, it rolled on across Nevada to keep on schedule. On the other side of state, the same train was boarded by a second, completely separate band of robbers. There wasn't much left to steal.

Finishing the Railroad

T he Central Pacific Railroad crosses the American River just downstream of the Capital City

I-80 bridge that goes from down-town to Cal Expo. The original wooden bridge was replaced with a steel bridge that later fell into the river, taking a loaded train with it. The present steel bridge has been successfully carrying trains since 1912. The railroad still travels on the same line across America and the Ames Tool Company is still in business.

The struggling railroad got four times as much financing from the federal government for building through the mountains as for building across the valley. Arcade Creek is a small creek you can jump across near Howe Avenue. The railroad got California geologists to declare that because the soil looked different on the north side of Arcade Creek, that is where the mountains be-gin—never mind that you can not see a hill for miles around. This profitable tall tale is marked by a monument at Haggin Oaks Golf Course.

The federal government had more important things to think about in the middle of the Civil War and the extra money plus better credit terms helped save the railroad. If you live east of

Howe Avenue you live in the Sierra Nevada mountains accord-ing to a railroad act signed by Abraham Lincoln.

Sacramento kept the Central Pacific running in the 1800's and 1900's with the largest manufac-turing plant west of the Missis-sippi located north of downtown Sacramento. Sacramento workers made everything from locomo-tives to lamps. A train that runs around Disneyland is modeled on a Sacramento designed en-gine. The railroad shops had a boss named Andrew Stevens who was so good to his workers that they built a monument to him which still stands in front of City Hall.

Sacramento and the Gold Country went from ox carts through the Pony Express and steam locomotives to the rockets of the space age in just over 100 years.

Trains cut through mountains that took the settlers weeks to climb. **SAMCC**

Chapter Nine

FIRE AND WATER

California became a full-grown state while one half of the world still doubted its existence.
JD Borthwick, 1857

Floods

The same river waters that bring gold can also bring destruction. Supercharged by melting snow in the winter and spring, the American, Sacramento, Bear, Yuba and Cosumnes rivers have flooded the valley for thousands of years. This was a good thing before settlers arrived: Indians and animals moved above the flood and the land got rich. Settlers stuck in permanent houses and businesses stayed put and got wet.

Sutter wanted to sell his land for money, but he had been around long enough to see a few floods in the very place where the 49ers were creating Sacramento. Sutter urged the settlers to build their town on higher land at a place he called Sutterville, near where the zoo is now around William Land Park. Instead, the pioneers chose to settle in the worst possible spot for flooding,

where the rivers come together in what is now called Old Sacramento. Sutter had used the site of Old Sacramento for a landing, but he had enough sense to build his fort on a slightly higher piece of ground, at today's 27th and K streets. Even so, visitors who came to the outpost between Christmas and New Year's in 1841 could land their boats just a few steps behind the fort on a slough Sutter had dredged almost to his door.

Early Sacramento was hit by floods in 1850, 1852, 1853, 1861, 1862, and 1867, and 1878. It can happen again, even with modern controls. In 1986, more than half the rain that usually falls in a year fell in less than two weeks, sending Folsom Lake into overflow. Water flowed in many city streets. Last ditch management of Folsom Dam and other flood control gates barely kept most houses from being flooded. Dams don't always work; in 1995 a broken spillway gate in Folsom Dam drained half of Folsom Lake, washing out part of the American River bike trail. Another near flood struck in 1997.

In the early days, 49ers had hardly settled in when the first big flood hit in January 1850. During December and January it rained hard and both the Sacramento and American Rivers rose, flooding the new City of Sacramento. Communication between Sacramento and the mining region to the east was cut off.

A young Swiss merchant, sick and frightened, was trapped on the top shelf in his store:

...tired of waiting and calling out, I resigned myself to spending a second night in company with the rats that seemed to be feasting on their sacks of flour. I follow suit and started to nibble on a few biscuits, but the fever had dulled my hunger.

Besides, I was suffering more from a lack of water than of food. To bring up water, all I had to do by then was to stretch out my arm, the level having risen about thirteen inches during the day so that it was only two and a half feet from me.

..If at daybreak the danger of being submerged had not passed, I had decided to break through the roof by attempting to raise one or two boards with my head, and then to straddle the peak and call and scream until a passerby might come and get me.

(Theophile de Rutte, 1850)

De Rutte was rescued, but as he recovered he witnessed a "strange spectacle":

The American Fork had carried and deposited everywhere in its path a gold-bearing silt, of little value it is true, but sufficiently rich to attract the attention of the city's inhabitants. Soon the entire population was transformed into as many miners, and everyone sought to procure for himself a dish, plate or cup to pan this silt, which, fortunately for businesses in danger of being abandoned, was paying from a day's washing a maximum of only two dollars ($40 in modern money), so that the Americans, little satisfied with such a small amount, wasted no time in returning to their usual occupations.

(de Rutte, 1850)

An early Sacramento physician wrote about a man called the Dutchman who earned thousands of dollars in gold dust ferrying the dead through the flood to burial sites.

The Dutchman always kept his gold dust on him. On one trip with a coffin and a helper, the

Sacramento flood cartoon. Some people said there were so many floods they should move the government. The State Capitol is built high above the water.

From: CSL

Dutchman's boat began to sink. While his helper clung to the coffin and was saved, the Dutchman was pulled under by the weight of his gold.

(Dr. John Morse, 1850)

130

"The city is one vast lake, and boats are busily engaged passing to and fro, conveying people in search of meals and lodging," wrote the Sacramento Bee in a "Flood Sheet" published while its own building was underwater.

The flood of 1862 covered an even wider area. William Brewer was writing in March, when most of the area had been under water for three months:

"The great central valley of the state is underwater, a region 250-300 miles long, and an average of 20 miles wide."

After the unhappy experience of 1850, Sacramentans had worked feverishly to build up dirt levee walls around the city. Unfortunately, during the early spring of 1852, continuous rains in the lowlands and heavy snows in the mountains caused the rivers to rise rapidly. The new levee broke near what is now Discovery Park. Desperate people threw dirt, bags of grain and even valuable building lumber into the break, but nothing could stop the water from churning through the city streets. Another major flood occurred at the end of the year, covering Sacramento City and the plains for miles around.

Wagons and mules coming down from the mountains could not get any closer than nine miles from Sacramento before they hit the flood. Miners starving for supplies and merchants who needed the miner's gold to pay bills were both worried sick until the first brave animals and men pushed their way through mud and water up to their waists.

Nine years later, near the beginning of the Civil War, new, supposedly safe levees broke again. The new railroad to Folsom couldn't make it into Sacramento. Water was as deep as five feet at the corner of 3rd and K Streets. At Folsom the water rose 60 feet above normal. The flood was so powerful that it destroyed every bridge on the American River between Folsom and Sacramento.

Indian people living near Marysville left their homes and went up into the foothills one week before this disastrous flood. Predicting an extraordinary deluge, they told the whites it would be higher than it had been for thirty years. Because of the high water, steamboats were able to go up the American River. But not for long; at the height of the flood the steamboat Gem got swept through a break in the levee and came to rest in an orchard near 23rd and B Streets.

Clearly Sacramento had a problem. One water engineer called the flood "a crashing muttering wave, carrying destruction to everything moveable".

This report reinforced what many a wet person already knew: if rivers were bowling alleys; Sacramento was sitting right in the middle of the pins. People couldn't move their houses, so they moved the channels of the rivers. The American was straightened so that it flows more directly into the Sacramento River. The Sacramento was given an emergency drain which allowed flooding to be swept into agricultural lands in Yolo County instead of into the State Capital. Just to make sure, the front doors of many older houses downtown are raised up to the second story like a lady lifting her skirts to get through a mud puddle. Even the State Capital and many whole downtown streets are built up high to avoid the very real possibility: it could flood again.

At first, the answer seemed to be to build higher levee walls to protect people and farms. Unfortunately, higher levees just made flooding worse because

132

Modern Sacramento is mostly fireproof and dry.
Photo: Tom Meyers.

The Great Fire burned most of Sacramento.
Fires were common in wooden towns lit by gas lamps
and candles.
Colorized. SAMCC.

River water irrigates one of the richest agricultural areas in the world. **Photo: Tom Meyers.**

they kept the water from spreading out. After storms, the river came down its narrow channel like a run- away freight train. Soil and rocks from hydraulic mining made the rivers run even higher. In Sacramento's first thirty years, floods got deeper and deeper. Each overflow scared citizens into building higher levees, which made the next flood worse.

Finally people begin to realize that levees alone are no solution to flood problems. Since you can't stop a river, engineers begin to dig canals that can carry flood water around towns and major farms. The road to San Francisco rides on stilts across the long Yolo Causeway so that water can safely flood land outside of towns. The Sacramento Weir is 48 gates in the levee which can be opened to send water west down the Sacramento Bypass under the Yolo Causeway. This has created a beautiful wetland that provides living space for thousands of birds.

Diversion canals, levees and dams are the main protections for today's Sacramento. While officials have to look out for an ever growing area of houses, land has been set aside without devel-

With planning, food and people can grow in the same area. **Photo: Tom Meyers.**

opment to allow for safe overflow when there is a flood. Hydraulic mining was outlawed over a hundred years ago so the rivers have had time to return to their natural channels. Even with preparation, there is no guarantee the rivers will stay in those channels if too much water tumbles out of the mountains. When you live in a river town, there is always the chance of getting wet.

Fires

With open flames for light and cooking, not to mention plenty of cigars, Gold Rush towns made of wood and canvas burned down regularly. San Francisco had so many fires that to this day its symbol is a phoenix, the legendary bird that rises from its own ashes. Fires burned most of Sacramento three times in the first five years. Flaming planks flew through the air driven by burning gusts of wind. The Governor called for volunteers, but about all they could save was a portrait of George Washington.

Placerville burned three times in one year. After that they ordered a bell to call the firefighters which still stands on a hundred year old tower in the middle of town. Auburn burned more than once until they built an amazing red and white three story Victorian firehouse; still the pride of old Auburn. Volunteer firefighters were proud of their outfits; sometimes rival companies would actually fight each other for the right to put out a fire.

Using the Rivers

Water can be trouble, but it is also as necessary as the air we breathe. The Sacramento area contains some of the richest agricultural land in the world even through not enough rain falls on the fields to grow most kinds of crops. These crops can grow because there is a steady supply of water brought from lakes through irrigation canals to farms and ranches. When a dam is built to hold up a river, a reservoir lake behind the dam stops water when there is too much and lets water go when there is not enough. Dams can overflow or run out of water, but they provide a safety zone in most water years.

There have been small dams at Folsom since the early days; one of them brought Sacramento the first long distance hydro-

electricity in the world. These dams were good enough for local power but not nearly big enough to store water for farmers or help protect Sacramento from floods. Then in the 1930's Sacramento saw the beginning of a project that would make even the water hungry gold miners gasp. The Central Valley Project sponsored by the U.S. government built the Folsom Dam and many others. The Project channeled water from Northern California rivers through Central Valley farms all the way to Los Angeles.

In the sixty years since its beginning the Project boasts that it has:

Circled the great valley with a necklace of majestic dams, wedged into the canyons of the Sierra and Coast Range. Primarily, the spacious reservoirs they have created are intended to hold runoff waters from the mountains surrounding the valley during the winter and spring and by dint of engineering marvels, drop these waters to the valley floor in measured installments during the hot summer months. The dams do other things besides. They prevent floods; they convert billions of tons of tamed torrents into electrical energy; they provide water to homes and industries ...

138

Nature consistently reminds mankind who really is in control with floods and dry periods. The Central Valley of California is a magnificent example of this. The Sacramento River watershed receives two-thirds of northern California's water though it only has one-third of the land. The San Joaquin River watershed occupies two-thirds of northern California's land, but only collects one-third of the rain. The Sacramento Valley suffers from floods, while the San Joaquin area often has no water at all. This is bad for both farmers and fish.

The new law in the 1990's made the Central Valley Project more environmental. The act took water away from farmers to be used to protect fish. The partial restoration of Mono Lake and the Owens River, once sucked almost dry by Los Angeles, is a step toward restoring the natural world in the mountains.

The Central Valley contains three-quarters of the irrigated land in California, and one-sixth of the irrigated land in the United States. The Central Valley's annual farm production exceeds the total value of all the gold mined in California since 1848.

The fight to stay dry and keep the water where it will do the most good for farms and nature is continuing. The Sacramento area is raising dams and levees while it works to protect the bubbling resource that brought it gold and people in the first place - clean running rivers.

The California State Capital. **Photo: Tom Meyers**

Chapter Ten
MAKING MONEY

**Been a great deal of hard times
as well as considerable prosperity...**

Joseph Pike, California fortune seeker

Sacramento is the capital of the Golden State. In the early years, earning a living meant either mining gold or mining the gold miners by selling something they wanted. Today, there are lots of different ways to make money.

John Sutter had a big head start as the original owner of most of Sacramento, but he lost his empire to fast talking businessmen in the rush for gold. He got so mad that he moved back east. There Sutter lived out his days comfortably enough, but he spent years trying to get the government to pay him back for what he lost in Sacramento. Sutter had good ideas, but he drank a lot and had trouble following his own plans. Neither he nor the Native Americans who once controlled all the land could stand up to the gold hungry swarm of settlers.

When they weren't too busy looking for gold, settlers loved bread, donuts and tortillas. To make them, wheat and corn had to be ground in mills. Sutter was building a food mill when the Gold Rush took away all his workers. Even in the middle of the Gold Rush, other businessmen managed to complete California's first water driven mill in Folsom. Mills got washed away in floods, but they were rebuilt immediately, because hungry miners were ready to pay plenty for food. Eventually steam power let the mills move away from the side of the periodically dangerous rivers.

Early Californians needed lots of leather for shoes and saddles. Fortunately, leather is made from the hides of cattle which were the main product of California before the Gold Rush. Since there were no refrigerators, ranchers let wild animals eat most of the meat, but they did make money selling hides. Hides were made into leather in a factory called a tannery. Sutter had the first tannery but he sold it to look for gold. Rabel's Tannery north of downtown Sacramento made good money for years turning hides into leather.

There were plenty of trees in Gold Country, but no way to cut them up into boards. Gold was actually discovered by Sutter's men working to build a saw mill to make boards for Sutter's other businesses. Once they found gold, all the people rushing to California needed wood for houses and mining. Sutter could not keep his saw mill working, but other people did. A few years into the Gold Rush, a steam powered saw mill was running in downtown Sacramento with logs floated down the American River. Sending logs down the river had to be stopped years later when they jammed up and guards at the new Folsom Prison started to worry that a dangerous prisoner might escape by clinging to a floating log.

Business buildings and streets in Sacramento, San Francisco and

Gladding McBean cast sculpture decorates buildings all over the U.S.
They still make it. **Photo: Tom Meyers**

Sacramento was an early home to movie making and music distribution around the world. It has always been hipper than it looks. **Photo: Tom Meyers.**

other towns in Northern California were built with granite and cobblestones mined in Folsom and the town named for stone: Rocklin. Even though stone was heavy, it could be shipped down the river in empty boats that had already delivered their load of supplies for the miners.

In 1874, the Gladding McBean Company began selling pipe plus beautiful terra cotta statues and decorative panels that became part of fancy buildings in San Francisco and other cities in the U.S. More than 100 years later, they still make these products. Whether stone or terra cotta, historic buildings all over America

often contain a bit of the Sacramento area.

In 1895 Sacramento staged an elaborate "Electric Carnival" to celebrate the world's first long-distance transmission of power, from a dam at Folsom to Sacramento. Like a Disneyland parade, twinkling floats passed under lighted arches and the Capitol glowed in incandescent glory that could be seen all the way into the foothills, (see Chapter 7). By today's standards the 22 miles from Folsom to Sacramento may not seem like much, but in 1895 no one in the world had tried to send electricity that far. So little was known about

Most of the early Air Force flew over Sacramento in war exercises.
Sacramento made planes and trained pilots. SAMCC.

electricity that people were afraid it might lose power going around corners, so builders kept the lines as straight as possible. Both the brick substation at 6th and H Streets where the power entered Sacramento and the power house at Folsom are still standing.

Taking over from those pioneering efforts, the Sacramento area is the home of the most environmentally-minded electrical utility company in the world.

The Sacramento Municipal Utility District (SMUD) is pub-

licly owned by the people who use it. SMUD took over electricity for the area after World War II, following a 20 year legal fight with a money-making electric company that did not want to give up the business. SMUD inherited a mess, without a single map of where the wires went. The first thing that went wrong is that the electricity blew out in their own office. After years of patient work, SMUD built an efficient system that uses non-polluting energy as much as possible. Many users voluntarily let their air conditioners be turned down for a few minutes when demand gets too high and pay a little extra to insure that the energy they use comes from clean renewable sources like hydroelectricity, wind, solar and biomass.

Aerospace

In World War I, the Liberty Iron Works in north Sacramento won a contract to build 150 Curtis "Jenny" biplanes a month. A whole generation of Americans learned to fly on Jennies, as did pilots in Canada, Great Britain and France. After the war, new civilian pilots bought thousand of the inexpensive planes and Jennies had a second career as a barnstorming plane, thrilling spectators at traveling air shows throughout the United States.

Sacramento was one of four Jenny plants in the United States. Since Sacramento was building so many early planes, it was a good place to train pilots for the Air Force. Between the World Wars, Sacramento was the center of a pretend war featuring almost the entire early United States air force (see picture). Mather Field was a major training base for 75 years, changing to a civilian air business park in 1995. McClellan Base fixed planes for the Air Force from World War II until returning to civilian life in 2001. In the early days, young pilots would show off by flying under the river bridges.

Sacramento joined the space age early. Aerojet General began building a rocket factory south of Folsom in 1951. In the 1950's and 60's, Aerojet was the largest rocket plant in the world. Now Aerojet makes other high tech products for the military. The McDonnell-Douglas Company's Sacramento Test Center spent the 1960's preparing Saturn rocket stages used in NASA's Apollo lunar landing. Like Aerojet, McDonnell-Douglas cut back on its activities at the Test Center in the 1970s, and the land has since become an industrial and residential area.

The two largest computer related manufacturers in the Sacramento area are Hewlett Packard in Roseville and Intel in Folsom.

HP makes printers and computers while Intel develops and manufactures the most popular line of computer processors in the world. Sacramento manufactures and develops computer equipment with over 25,000 area workers employed in high tech.

State Government

As capital of the largest population state, Sacramento has more than 150,000 government jobs; about 28% of all employees in the area work for the state. This steady base of employment has kept the region stronger during economic downturns than many other parts of the state and nation.

Agriculture

California agriculture makes more money in one year than all the gold ever mined in the state because California combines rich land with careful management of water and crops. Two hundred years ago the Central Valley around Sacramento was a seasonal wetland with a wonderful world of wild plants and animals, but no crops. The change to more food and less nature started with John Sutter.

John Sutter was the first rancher in the American River area and he had big plans. He told early visitors he was going to export grain, vegetables, butter and cheese. Where he was going to sell all this was a little unclear, since in early California it was thousands of miles to the nearest city. Sutter also dreamed about growing rice, cotton, indigo dye, grapes, olives and other fruit. With the exceptions of cotton and indigo, all his agricultural dreams have come true, even though they did not come true for him.

146

Here is how John Bidwell who worked for Sutter described the wheat harvest before the Gold Rush:

Imagine three or four hundred ... Indians in a grain field, armed, some with sickles, some with butcher knives, some with pieces of hoop iron roughly fashioned like sickles, but many having only their hands with which to gather by small handfuls the dry and brittle grain...

But the wildest part was the thrashing... three or four hundred wild horses were turned in to thrash it, the Indians whooping to make them run faster...

Pears from gold country.
Photo: Tom Meyers

Even before the Gold Rush year of 1849 was over, a far-sighted pioneer named A.P. Smith was planting a farm in Sacramento. Located across the river from what is now Cal Expo, Smith had 90 acres of fruit and vegetables for immediate sale to hungry miners plus seeds that helped other farmers get crops going. He had beauty as well as food: 15,000 roses and the flower that would become the symbol of Sacramento: winter blooming camellias. Smith was high tech for the time, using a steam engine to pump river water into a tower tank from which pipes ran to the plants. Two miles of paths paved with white seashells from San Francisco wound through the garden. Without tractors or agricultural chemicals, it took 30 people working year round to keep his garden growing.

The miners liked food, but they did not put up with farmers getting in the way of their hunt for gold. In 1851 they shot a farmer in the south foothills whose irrigation system was spilling into their mining claim. Then they tore down his dam. Other miners in the north foothills pushed their way through the fence around a hay field and dug so many prospecting holes that the crop was ruined.

Farmers fought back. James Warren set up a nursery business in Sacramento and lobbied until the legislature established a state agricultural society. With California too busy mining gold to grow its own food, a speaker dared to say:

If the mines should suddenly fail.... we would not only be a happier and better people but in a few years richer and stronger... The gamblers and loafers would instantly take their flight...there would remain here men of character and substance...with such a population as this, devoted to the peaceful pursuit of agriculture, California would quickly become the garden spot of the world.

On its way to becoming the world's garden spot, California decided to stop for a drink. Grape vine planting was well established a few years into the Gold Rush with the Sacramento area far ahead of Napa Valley in the amount of wine it made. In the early days California wine was pretty bad, but it was cheap by Gold Rush standards: about $4.00 in modern money for a gallon. The miners drank a lot. In addition to local wine, Californians, who made up only 1

The area grows most varieties of grapes. **Photo: Tom Meyers.**

There are lots of different grape growers. **Photo: Tom Meyers**

percent of the U.S. population at the time, consumed more than 25 percent of all imported alcoholic beverages.

By twenty years after the gold discovery, the Central Valley was not only producing enough flour to make bread for everyone in California, it was exporting ship loads of wheat all over the world.

For a few years, wheat was the new gold, harvested for a quick profit by huge machines pulled by platoons of horses or even early steam tractors. It may not have been the best crop for California in the long run, but it helped local agriculture break into world markets and catch up with the profits from gold. When the railroad was completed across the country after the Civil War, more and more kinds of California food could reach eastern buyers.

The area near present day CSUS was once the sweet tooth capital of California with hundreds of acres of sugar beets and a factory six stories high producing 100 tons of sugar a day. Nor was sugar the only thrill; two distilleries made brandy from local sugar and grapes. Hop fields helped several Sacramento breweries turn out wagon loads of beer.

On the Haggin Ranch that stretched from east Sacramento to what is now Carmichael,

thoroughbred horses ran. In the 1880's, a Sacramento horse named Ben Ali won the Kentucky Derby and Haggin horses overall won more race money then any stable in the country.
The horses made way for houses in the early 1900's.

Although cities have grown, crops still make up half of the land area and one out of every twenty dollars in income.

The Sacramento and the Gold Country still have room to grow food along with jobs and people.

However, the river lands from downtown Sacramento to Fair Oaks continued to be used mostly for growing food until after World War II.
Hop fields, vegetable gardens and orchards grew on the rich river front land all the way from Sacramento to the river bluffs near Folsom. Vegetable gardens were closest to the city with carefully tended fields and orchards beyond.

In the early 21st century, hops for beer are grown elsewhere but grapes for wine still make up about a third of crop income and Gold Country wineries are getting famous again. On area ranches you can find pears, corn, rice, turkeys, tomatoes and cattle.

Adventure Tour

Welcome to the heart of the Gold Rush, the Pony Express, the Transcontinental Railroad and the California Republic. Pioneers wanted to keep it simple, so the streets go 1, 2, 3 starting with 1st Street (also called Front Street) at the River. Cross streets go A, B, C from north to south.

1. Black Railroad Bridge (I Street)
Even though it carries the main railroad line across the United States, this bridge can swing its whole self around in the middle to let boats through. You can see both bridges from the Delta King.

2. California Railroad Museum (2nd and I Streets)
Check out sleek old trains, gleaming like when they carried the pioneers. One of the best railroad museums in the world. See the orientation film first; it drops you right into the Transcontinental Railroad adventure.

9. Delta King (K and Front Streets, Sacramento River)
This paddlewheel boat carried people to San Francisco - check out the colored glass river trip in the upstairs lounge at the front of the boat. The King's Sacramento River sister, the Delta Queen, sailed to the Mississippi where it reenacts the days of Mark Twain. Speaking of Mark Twain, he walked past the spot where you are standing on his way to write for the Sacramento Union.

8. Old Sacramento (everything between the River and 2nd Street from I to L Streets)
Walk into history. The Pony Express and Wells Fargo stage coaches started at 2nd and J Streets. Facing down an insurrection, the first mayor of Sacramento was shot at 4th and J; the next day the sheriff was killed in a gun battle (see Chapter 6). The corner of Front and J Streets where miners bought gold pans at Sam Brannan's store is now home to Fat City's Tiffany stained glass and the bar on which the Unsinkable Molly Brown poured drinks.

7. Golden Tower Bridge (M Street, usually called Capitol Mall)
Tower Bridge goes up in the middle to let big boats through. Neither the original Pony Express nor the Transcontinental Railroad went to San Francisco. They didn't have to: riverboats carried everybody on a sometimes wild overnight cruise in the early days.

3. Sculpture Garden (12th and K Streets)
Over 100 feet of blue neon glows like a psychic beacon over nighttime Sacramento. At its foot, fountains and sculpture from ancient Greek to modern funny. A naked Poseidon statue from 400 BC was too sexy for a convention of fundamentalists. Every morning they put pants on the statue and every day outraged artists snuck in and pulled the pants down. Poseidon remains as proudly naked as the day he was first carved 2500 years ago.

4. California State Capitol (10th and L Streets)
Home to governors like Earl Warren, Ronald Reagan and Arnold Schwarzenegger. The Speaker of the Assembly called the inner rotunda "psychedelic" when it was restored along with the rest of the Capitol to 1800's grandeur. Senate and the Assembly chambers are almost too beautiful to pass laws in. Displays from each of California's 58 counties make a mini state tour in the hallways. Check out the seismograph past the Governor's Office near the back door for an instant earthquake report. Capitol Park has weird and wonderful trees, flowers and oranges.

6. Old City Cemetery (9th and Broadway, old Y Street)
Some people feel ghosts. Mark Hopkins, one of the Big Four builders of the railroad, lies in a striking pink mausoleum. May Woolsey died as a child. A hundred years later, they found a letter in the old Woolsey house that seemed to come from beyond the grave. Visitors claim you can still feel her presence, literally, by holding your hand near her grave stone. Other permanent residents include the mayor shot in the Squatters Riot, John Sutter, Jr., an engineer who died at the controls of his train trying to save his passengers, and an infamous cannibal from the Donner Party (Chapter 4).

5. Sutter's Fort (27th and L Streets)
Sutter's Fort made the Gold Rush happen. You can still feel the frontier behind its walls. Check out living history days when the Fort comes alive with mountain men and settlers. Just outside, the California Indian Museum sits under ancient trees

To The Gold
Old Folsom. Coloma Gold Discovery Site. Placerville Gold Bug Mine. Auburn Courthouse Gold Collection. Grass Valley Empire Mine. Grass Valley, Malakoff Diggins.

Adventure Tour

Welcome to the heart of the Gold Rush, the Pony Express, the Transcontinental Railroad and the California Republic. Pioneers wanted to keep it simple, so the streets go 1, 2, 3 starting with 1st Street (also called Front Street) at the River. Cross streets go A, B, C from north to south.

1. Black Railroad Bridge (I Street)
Even though it carries the main railroad line across the United States, this bridge can swing its whole self around in the middle to let boats through. You can see both bridges from the Delta King.

2. California Railroad Museum (2nd and I Streets)
Check out sleek old trains, gleaming like when they carried the pioneers. One of the best railroad museums in the world. See the orientation film first; it drops you right into the Transcontinental Railroad adventure.

9. Delta King (K and Front Streets, Sacramento River)
This paddlewheel boat carried people to San Francisco - check out the colored glass river trip in the upstairs lounge at the front of the boat. The King's Sacramento River sister, the Delta Queen, sailed to the Mississippi where it reenacts the days of Mark Twain. Speaking of Mark Twain, he walked past the spot where you are standing on his way to write for the Sacramento Union.

8. Old Sacramento (everything between the River and 2nd Street from I to L Streets)
Walk into history. The Pony Express and Wells Fargo stage coaches started at 2nd and J Streets. Facing down an insurrection, the first mayor of Sacramento was shot at 4th and J; the next day the sheriff was killed in a gun battle (see Chapter 6). The corner of Front and J Streets where miners bought gold pans at Sam Brannan's store is now home to Fat City's Tiffany stained glass and the bar on which the Unsinkable Molly Brown poured drinks.

3. Sculpture Garden (12th and K Streets)
Over 100 feet of blue neon glows like a psychic beacon over nighttime Sacramento. At its foot, fountains and sculpture from ancient Greek to modern funny. A naked Poseidon statue from 400 BC was too sexy for a convention of fundamentalists. Every morning they put pants on the statue and every day outraged artists snuck in and pulled the pants down. Poseidon remains as proudly naked as the day he was first carved 2500 years ago.

7. Golden Tower Bridge (M Street, usually called Capitol Mall)
Tower Bridge goes up in the middle to let big boats through. Neither the original Pony Express nor the Transcontinental Railroad went to San Francisco. They didn't have to: riverboats carried everybody on a sometimes overnight cruise in the early days.

4. California State Capitol (10th and L Streets)
Home to governors like Earl Warren, Ronald Reagan and Arnold Schwarzenegger. The Speaker of the Assembly called the inner rotunda "psychedelic" when it was restored along with the rest of the Capitol to 1800's grandeur. Senate and the Assembly chambers are almost too beautiful to pass laws in. Displays from each of California's 58 counties make a mini state tour in the hallways. Check out the seismograph past the Governor's Office near the back door for an instant earthquake report. Capitol Park has weird and wonderful trees, flowers and oranges.

6. Old City Cemetery (9th and Broadway, old Y Street)
Some people feel ghosts. Mark Hopkins, one of the Big Four builders of the railroad, lies in a striking pink mausoleum. May Woolsey died as a child. A hundred years later, they found a letter in the old Woolsey house that seemed to come from beyond the grave. Visitors claim you can still feel her presence, literally, by holding your hand near her grave stone. Other permanent residents include the mayor shot in the Squatters Riot, John Sutter, Jr., an engineer who died at the controls of his train trying to save his passengers, and an infamous cannibal from the Donner Party (Chapter 4).

5. Sutter's Fort (27th and L Streets)
Sutter's Fort made the Gold Rush happen. You can still feel the frontier behind its walls. Check out living history days when the Fort comes alive with mountain men and settlers. Just outside, the California Indian Museum sits under ancient trees

To The Gold
Old Folsom. Coloma Gold Discovery Site. Placerville Gold Bug Mine. Auburn Courthouse Gold Collection. Grass Valley Empire Mine. Grass Valley, Malakoff Diggins.

Chapter Eleven
GROWING UP BEAUTIFUL

**Here is a climate that breeds vigour,
with just sufficient geniality to prevent the expenditure of most
of that vigour in fighting the elements.**
Jack London

By the end of the 1800's, the gold craze died down enough for people to notice that California was a beautiful place to live. Shivering easterners dreamed about palm trees and orange groves. Settlers bought 10 acre plots and grew oranges and olives.

Between the Gold Rush and today, the number of people who call Sacramento and the Gold Country home has doubled almost every 10 years. In the 2000's, the river and foothill area had the 22nd largest population in the United States. It is a city without many of the urban blues, made up of towns and green space that combine to make a place for people.

Diversity

In the early days of the Gold Rush, Sarah Carroll went to the police because her money, jewelry and best clothes had been stolen from the room she rented in downtown Sacramento. Police arrested the thief but they had to let him go because Sarah Carroll's skin was dark. In the verdict of the court: "Defendant (the thief) was discharged, he proving himself a white man and none but colored testimony against him."

Until the 1860's, California law allowed white people to get away with crimes because Indians and people who were even partly black could not legally testify against white people. Chinese and other minorities got the hardest jobs and the worst treatment. Despite the legal thievery, Sarah Carroll did not give up. She lived to see the unfair law repealed and to own her own house in Sacramento.

It took years, but gradually people in California learned to work together. According to a

Harvard University study of the 2000 census data, Sacramento has become the most diverse city in the United States.

In this area, everybody is a minority: 41 percent are white, 22 percent are called Hispanic, 17.5 percent are Asian and 15.5 percent are African American.

Even more important, Sacramento is the most integrated city; people of different backgrounds live near each other, work, play and go to school together. While there is still a long way to go, the city by the rivers has shown that people that come from different backgrounds can live together successfully.

The Sacramento Kings

The Sacramento Kings brought major league basketball to the area in 1985. In the early years they were terrible, but loyal fans sold out the arena for every game. At one time the Kings had the longest losing record in professional sports and, at the same

The Sacramento Kings. **Photo: Tom Myers**

time, one of the longest continuous records of sold out games. All this cheering support paid off in the 2000's as the Kings became national contenders, not because of any one star, but based on teamwork and lightening offense.

Famous Governors

If it were a country instead of a state, California would have the 7th richest economy in the world. Since California includes Hollywood as well as high tech, agriculture, beautiful nature and the most people in the United States, it makes sense that the government in Sacramento attracts some famous people.

Leland Stanford was conveniently governor and president of the track building Central Pacific Railroad at the same time during the Civil War.

Governor Arnold Schwarzenegger. **Photo: Tom Meyers**

Earl Warren was a popular governor who made important case law as Chief Justice of the US Supreme Court in the mid-1900's. Richard Nixon was elected both Vice President and President twice, but California refused to elect him governor even once in between these two national offices.

Ronald Reagan was in more than 50 movies before he was elected governor of California by big margins twice, starting in 1966. He had been president of the Hollywood Screen Actor Guild and a popular host on television. A conservative Republican who was liked even by people who disagreed with him, he was elected President by landslide votes twice beginning in 1980.

He had been President for only a few weeks when he was wounded by a crazy gunman. As he was being wheeled into the hospital, he reportedly said to the surgeon, "I hope you are not a Democrat". He recovered quickly and went on to strongly continue the 50 year US opposition to Communism called the cold war until Communist power ended after his administration.

Arnold Schwarzenegger was a weight lifter from Europe called "The Austrian Oak" who won every important body building competition so often he became the most important man in the history of the sport. He came to California, got a college degree and went from managing workout studios to being an action hero movie star. The simple tough guy he played in movies such as *The Terminator, Total Recall* and *True Lies* led one critic to say that his acting range stretched "*from A almost to B*". Schwarzenegger was, however, smarter than he looked.

After heading physical fitness programs for both the California and the US, Schwarzenegger won a recall election for Governor by a landslide. Although a Republican, he was married to a member of the famous Democrat Kennedy family and supported many social issues.

As Governor, he got voter approval to deal with a large budget shortfall and require balanced spending. He also achieved long overdue reform of the state program to help injured workers. He was a California Governor as famous as his state.

As a city of towns, the Sacramento area continues to grow.

Orangevale

Orange Vale Colony started out as 10 acre lots neatly divided by streets every half mile from north to south and every quarter

Fair Oaks

When Fair Oaks started around 1900, the advertising brochure said:

Life is precious; why court pneumonia, consumption and death in this climate of the East Coast when, at a moderate cost, you can secure an ideal home and a sure income in Fair Oaks.

Fair Oaks. TM

mile from east to west. In the 1800's thousands of orange trees were planted but orange trees have trouble in Sacramento winters that are colder than normal. An early publicity pamphlet that said Orange Vale had a climate even better than that of the Mediterranean Riviera was not totally lying; the Riviera can be cold in winter too.

Visitors were given a poem:
Ah, who would not live beyond the reach of the snows, Mid the fragrance of orange, lemon and rose,
With the almond and olive and vine on the lea, In the summer land breeze late kissed by the sea,
Where all of nature's bounties are fairest and free?

Buyers were promised a healthy climate and to prove it they could meet a local Indian who was said to be 136 years old. The first Fair Oaks residents really were living in the country. They passed only a few houses on their way to Sacramento. Getting downtown and back could take all day. The area started to grow after World War II.

Carmichael

A puff piece for Carmichael appeared in Sunset magazine in the early 1900's:

Carmichael Colony is advantageously situated in the shelter of the rolling foot-hills, secure from frosts...

Fortunes have been made and are being made here in the culture of citrus fruits... The [river and] woods hereabouts are stocked with trout for rod and ducks for gun. The climate insures the maximum of health-giving qualities and the temperature allows outdoor sleeping every night of the year. ...the owner of a tract may be as independent as a king in his castle. Eternal summer—no snow—no frost—no cyclones— no sunstrokes. We have our rainy season in the winter which corresponds to the snow season back East—this however, is not a drawback but a blessing.

Early settlers could borrow the money they needed to live until the harvest came in. Then they repaid the loan with no interest, always having a drink with the lender to celebrate. No fortunes were made in citrus trees but residents did have plenty of room to roam until housing took off in the 1950's.

Folsom Prison

There were far more criminals than prison cells to hold them during the 1800's. California's only prison was San Quentin, full to overflowing, until Folsom Prison opened in 1880. A local company gave the state land for a prison in exchange for free convict labor to build a small early Folsom dam.

Granite for the prison was cut from the hills right where the cells were built. The original building with 324 cells is still in use more than 100 years later. The prison was built with two stories of cells each separated by stone walls a foot thick. Doors were solid iron with an opening the size of a mail slot for ventilation. The two prisoners in each cell had wooden bunks, straw mattresses, and two buckets—one for drinking and the other for a toilet. Oil lamps worked for both light and heat until the prison got electricity.

When the prison was only a few years old, prisoners took the warden hostage and made the guards turn over their weapons. The escaped criminals fought a battle with lawmen at Pilot Hill. Most were captured but their leader and four others were never seen again. There have been few escapes from Folsom Prison since a granite wall was built all around the cell block.

Additional cells were added over the years with a major new cell block completed in 1986. By 1990 the population had risen to 7,000 divided into two separate prison units.

River Park

Sacramento expanded to River Park after World War II. The developers who bought it found out there was a little problem because the American River had once flowed thorough the land.

Over the years the river had shifted making room for houses. The old map showed a river and that meant it was supposed to be under water and therefore under federal control. Once the Feds realized this land was no longer a river, the state claimed it. Finally the courts said the developers owned what they had bought and houses started to go up. The area grew in the 1950's with the beginning of California State University, Sacramento.

Auburn. TM

Rancho Cordova

Rancho Cordova is another area where farm land was subdivided for residences after WW II. In the old days the area was known as Mills and grew grapes for wine and hops for beer. Rancho Cordova is named for Cordova Vineyards. Streets like Zinfandel Drive remember the different grapes once grown in the area. The grand opening of the subdivision in 1953 featured early TV star Art Linkletter.

Auburn

Initially called North Fork Dry Diggings when a Frenchman discovered gold in 1848, it was renamed Auburn (after Auburn, N.Y.), and became a crossroads of the northern mines on the main line of the Central Pacific Railroad. Would be miners were actually on their way to the gold discovery site of Coloma when one of them found three gold nuggets while he was just trying out his new mining pan. Trails to the surrounding mines led out from Auburn, making it the center for stage and freight traffic.

Broderick

When the town was laid out in 1850 it was called Washington. About 1890, when residents petitioned for a post office, it was renamed Broderick. The name honors the memory of anti-slavery U.S. Sen. David C. Broderick killed near San Francisco in a suspicious duel with pro-slavery Judge David S. Terry in 1859.

Citrus Heights

Like its neighbor Orangevale, Citrus was the site of the early days of the citrus fruit industry

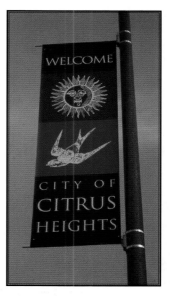

Citrus Heights. **Photo: Tom Meyers**

159

Festival in the Park. **Photo: Tom Meyers**

when it was a popular dream to own an orange grove in California. It turned out oranges need southern California's warm winters to grow in large numbers. Citrus Heights became a city in 1997.

Davis

Once called Davisville and named for Jerome C. Davis, rancher and landholder of the 1850s. Davis had been an explorer with John Fremont before he settled down and built a rope tow ferry to cross the river from Sacramento. He got his father to come out from Ohio and show him how to grow crops. Now the University of California, Davis shows the world how to grow crops (and minds) on the same land Jerome C. Davis once plowed.

Del Paso Heights

Rancho Del Paso was once the world's largest horse breeding ranch and home to a Kentucky Derby winner in 1886.

Elk Grove

James Hall, who came to California and opened a hotel in 1850, named the place for the Missouri town where he had lived. By 1876, the town sported two hotels, a flour mill and a number of businesses. In the Indian days, there once were really elk in the area.

El Dorado Hills

The entrance to the Gold Country on Highway 50, El Dorado Hills is named after a mythical land where where gold and precious stones are as common as rocks and wine flows gently from fountains. The name mean "the gilded one" in Spanish and was a long time dream of early explorers.

Folsom

Folsom was laid out in 1855 by Theodore Judah, the engineering brains of the Central Pacific Railroad, as the eastern terminus of the earlier Sacramento Valley Railroad. Judah took on the task for Capt. Joseph L. Folsom, a West Point graduate who came to San Francisco in 1847 and unfortunately died just when his city was getting started. Later Judah died just when the Central Pacific was getting started.

El Dorado Hills. **Photo: Tom Meyers**

161

Florin

In 1864 art loving Judge E. B. Crocker named this place for the abundance of beautiful wild flowers that grew there. The name was passed on to the small village that was an important fruit-shipping point on the Central Pacific Railroad starting in 1874.

Franklin

Founded by Andrew George who built the Franklin House there in 1856, the Franklin Cemetery holds the grave of Alexander Hamilton Willard, one of the last surviving members of the Lewis and Clark Expedition (1804-06).

Galt

The name goes back to John Galt, a Scottish novelist who set an example of realistic honesty. Along with Isleton, Folsom, Citrus Heights, Elk Grove and Rancho Cordova, it is one of the six small cities in Sacramento County.

Lincoln

Named for Col. Charles Lincoln Wilson, builder of the California Central Railroad (Folsom to Lincoln), the town first was settled in 1859. The discovery of an excellent bed of coal in 1873 first helped build the town. Clay samples taken from the coal mine in 1875 by A.J. Gladding led to the establishment of the Gladding-McBean earthware plant still in business in 2005.

Locke

Tin Sin Chan founded this Chinese community on the Sacramento River around 1916 after a suspicious fire destroyed the Chinatown in neighboring Walnut Grove. Land owner George

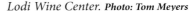

Lodi Wine Center. **Photo: Tom Meyers**

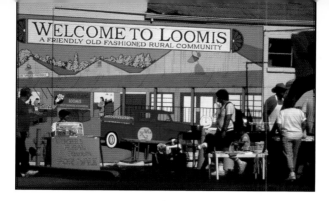

Loomis Mural. **Photo: Tom Meyers**

Locke gave his Chinese American neighbors room to build on his land. Locke is on the registry of national historical places because it is the only town in the United States built exclusively by the Chinese for the Chinese. It still looks about the way it did in 1920.

Lodi

Lodi, in Italy, was the scene of Napoleon's first spectacular victory in 1796. By the 1870s, more than 20 cities in this country had adopted the name. Lodi now has more than 50 wineries growing more kinds of grapes than Napa Valley.

Loomis

James Loomis ran a saloon where railroad men liked to have a few drinks. He would probably be amused that his former tough guy location now draws families from all over to the annual Eggplant Festival. Loomis does not grow that many eggplants, but they can taste good and all the other vegetables already had their own festivals.

Loomis Eggplant Festival.
Photo: Tom Meyers

Marysville

As a 13-year-old survivor of the Donner Party without a mother or father, Mary Murphy

Nevada City. **Photo: Tom Meyers**

felt she had to marry a 46-year-old drunk in order to survive. He treated her badly; she escaped, got divorced and married an honest farmer north of Sacramento. He named his new town after her. Years later her brother, who was only 11 when most of his family died in the snow, returned to the town named for his sister and became the city attorney. Marysville was a major supply town for the northern gold mines.

Newcastle

Originally known as Castle for a man who established a store and an inn near the mines in Secret Ravine, the place was rebuilt to be near the Central Pacific Railroad. Residents soon designated the growing community as "New Castle." A school district was formed in 1864 and the town became a prominent fruit-packing and shipping point.

Ophir

The only survivor of five mining camps named by literate forty-niners after Ophir, the land of gold mentioned frequently in the Bible. The place was known

Courthouse, Auburn. **Photo: Tom Meyers**

164

Fly in homes with air plane parking, Cameron Park.
Photo: Tom Meyers

as Spanish Corral in 1849, but it took the biblical name after a rich lode was unearthed in the area. It is a registered California historical landmark.

Placerville

Known as Dry Diggings by December of 1848, the historic mining camp was given the nickname Hangtown after two Frenchmen and a Chilean were hanged for stealing in 1849. In April 1851, a post office was established with the more polite name Placerville after the placer stream mining that went on in the area.

Rio Vista

This Solano County town was founded in 1857. It was origi-

Rocklin High School. **Photo: Tom Meyers**

nally called Brazos del Rio (arms of the river) because of its proximity to the junction of Cache Slough, Steamboat Slough and the Sacramento River. The name was changed to Rio Vista in 1860.

Rocklin

The name given to the station when the Central Pacific Railroad built the line from Sacramento to Newcastle in 1864 doubtless was suggested by all the granite rocks quarried in the area.

Roseville. **Photo: Tom Meyers**

Roseville

The story goes that the name was chosen by residents for the most popular girl at a picnic when the Central Pacific Railroad reached the spot in the spring of 1864. The city has been busy planting roses ever since.

Balloons go up, Serrano. **Tom Meyers**

Denio's Farmers Market, Roseville. **Tom Meyers**

Shingle Springs

Gold was discovered there in 1848. In 1849, a shingle mill was established and the mining camp took the name Shingle Springs. Several rich mines operated in the area as late as the 1930s.

Sloughhouse

Named after the hotel called the Slough House built in 1850 near a branch of the Cosumnes River.

Walnut Grove

Settled by woodcutters in the early 1850s, this rich region of once flooded river delta became a major shipping point for produce from the region's farms and orchards.

Woodland

The site was settled before 1855 as a trading post. When a post office was opened in 1859, it was named Woodland by the man who took over the store. The city's early importance is suggested by two architectural monuments, the Gable family mansion (1885) and the restored Opera House (1895).

Yuba City

Across the river from Marysville, Yuba City started out smaller but grew with agriculture and became the county seat. Yuba is the Indian word for both wild grapes and their local tribe.

Rich agricultural land.
Photo: Tom Meyers

169

Chapter Twelve
A NATURAL FUTURE

I only went out for a walk, and finally concluded to stay out till sundown, for going out, I found, was really going in.
John Muir,
California Nature Explorer

For thousands of years this place where the rivers meet between the mountains and the ocean has been rich with nature. In many ways, it still is.

Salmon may not fill the river as they did in Indian times, but there are still thousands of them and with careful management, more may be on the way. Grizzly bears no longer hunt along the streams, but deer, wild turkeys, coyotes and even an occasional mountain lion do. The sky is sometimes full of cranes, geese and other migrating birds. Year around there are great blue heron, egrets and the world's only yellow beaked magpies.

A young Swiss visitor reported how Gold Rush settlers gathered salmon:

I wondered where I would find breakfast, when I saw a flotilla of whaleboats

Wildflowers in gold country.
Photo: Tom Meyers

arrive, each carrying four men. They were salmon trawlers returning from a night of fishing. Their catch was abundant because each ship was carrying all

170

Salmon spawn up the American River. **DFG.**

it could hold. The population of the city of Sacramento at that time consisted only of about 1,500 people, and the catch consisted of more than 5,000 fish, each weighing six to eight pounds.

Even if each inhabitant managed to eat an entire one for his meal, I wondered what was going to be done with the rest of the take. This question was answered for me when I saw a group of men arriving with barrels and sacks of salt, who begin straight away to gut the fish, salt them, and lay them layer by layer in barrels. Once the latter were nailed shut, a cart carried them off to the mines, where the delicate pink flesh of the salmon is a great favorite.

(Theophile de Rutte, 1850)

Before there were dams, salmon spawned over 160 miles on all the forks of the American River up into the mountains. Salmon Falls above Folsom got its name from thousands of leaping fish. No more. Now Natomas and Folsom dams box the salmon in to only their first and most important spawning area. Before the dams, there were more than 100,000 fall run salmon. In the worst years of pollution and hydraulic mining debris, there were only about 5,000 fish left.

Amazingly enough, with careful management, the salmon have come back. Salmon runs are back to at least half of what they were in the old days and this goes on in the middle of one of the largest metropolitan areas in the United States. Along with Folsom Dam, the government built the Nimbus Fish Hatchery to help replace lost spawning beds. At the hatchery, fish leap up a stepped concrete waterfall called a fish ladder. At the top of the latter, eggs are removed from the females and sperm from the males. The eggs hatch in trays and young fish are raised in concrete ponds until they are ready to be released. Thousands of people watch the fish jump up their ladder and attend the annual Salmon Festival.

Salmon still spawn naturally in the eddies of the American River between the Watt and Hazel bridges. Naturally born salmon are three times as likely to survive in the wild as hatchery fish. Using senses that science still does not understand, salmon return from hundreds of miles at sea to the very place where they were born. When the runs of shad and striped bass are added to those of salmon and steelhead, the result is year-round fishing in Sacramento area rivers.

If an Indian and a Gold Rush miner could be transported through time to see that there are parks along their golden rivers through miles of modern city, they would be amazed for different reasons. To the Indian, everything was sacred and to the miner nothing could get in the way of the hunt for gold.

Mother and baby sheep. **Photo: Tom Meyers**

The American River Parkway is one of the largest natural areas in any city in the world, bigger than San Francisco's Golden Gate Park and New York's Central Park put together. The Parkway borders the river for 30 miles with trees, meadows and bike trails from Folsom Lake at the foot of the Sierra to the spot where the Sacramento and American rivers come together near Old Sacramento.

The Yuba River State Park covers 20 miles of swimming holes and rapids near historic gold mines in Nevada County. A North Fork American River Trail is planned to continue progress toward an eventual path over the mountains from Sacramento all the way to Nevada. Gold Country parks meet national forests that leave the region with more open space than city.

The rivers helped protect their banks by flooding regularly. Private land owners who controlled almost all the land along the rivers were afraid to build houses that might float away. Some land along the river was farmed or dredged for gold. Still, a lot of natural wildlife was preserved and people who felt it was part of their homeland wanted public ownership, not private gates.

When the wealthy Charles Goethe proposed to activist Mary Glide early in the 1900's, she said she would marry him only if he devoted his life to service for others. Their work together is remembered in the donation of woodland on the south bank of the American River in Goethe Park. The park is not named for the famous German philosopher, as many a visiting scholar has learned to their disappointment. But it is named for a generosity and love of nature which Johann Goethe would have heartily approved.

Ancil Hoffman Park on the north side of the river contains both a top rated public golf course and 77 acres of natural forest that is the home of the Effie Yeaw Nature Center. Ancil Hoffman was a county official who had been manager of Max Baer, Sacramento's only World Heavyweight Boxing Champion.

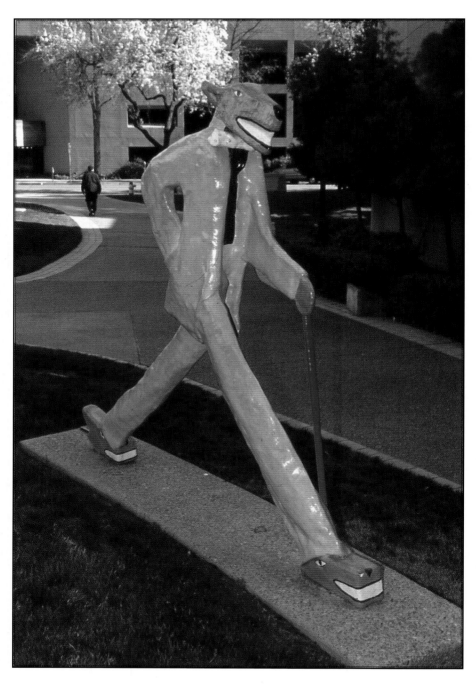

Walking the dogs, Sculpture Garden. American Indian/Chicano artist Gilbert "Magú" Luján made "Walking the Dog", in the Sculpture Garden near the Sacramento Convention Center (see Adventure Tour.)
Photo: Tom Meyers

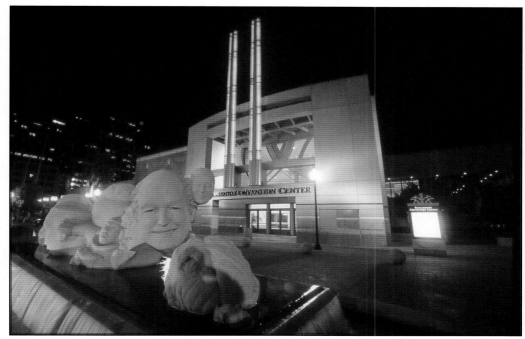

Convention, Sculpture Garden.
Photo: Tom Meyers

Climbing Wall. **Photo: Tom Meyers**

Reenactors at Sutter's Fort. **Photo: Tom Meyers**

Discovery Park, where the American River joins the Sacramento, has a boat launching ramp and beach. The Jedediah Smith Bike Path connects the whole parkway with a smooth two lane trail that goes over the same land Jedediah risked his life to explore almost 200 years ago.

On a bluff under an oak tree that has been growing since the days of the Indians, with the setting sun glowing golden over a clear river in which salmon jump, near a shore where deer and wild turkeys are common; it's good to remember that the tree shaded homes of millions of people are nearby.

Maybe people and nature can learn to live together. If so, that would be true gold.

Bears sometimes wait for salmon to jump before they grab them.
This dream-like picture of the past and the possible future is from the Great Wall
of Carmichael in Carmichael Park by local artist Hugh Gorman

Stone, Irving. Men to match my mountains: the opening of the far west, 1840-1900]. Special library ed. Newport Beach, CA

Delano, Alonzo. [2d thousand]. Life on the plains and among the diggings: being scenes and adventures of an overland journey to California: with particular incidents of the route, mistakes and sufferings of the emigrants, the Indian tribes, the present and future of the great West. Auburn: Milner, Orton & Mulligan, 1854.

Davis, William Heath. Seventy-five years in California: a history of events and life in California, personal, political and military, under the Mexican regime, during the quasi-military government of the territory by the United States, and after the admission of the state to the union. California collectors' ed. / San Francisco: J. Howell, 1929.

Severson, Thor. Sacramento: an illustrated history: 1839 to 1874, from Sutter's Fort to Capital City. Bicentennial reprint ed. [San Francisco]: California Historical Society, 1973.

California Indians I [-VI]. American Indian ethnohistory: California and Basin-Plateau Indians. New York: Garland Pub. Inc., 1974.

Bryant, Edwin. What I saw in California: being the journal of a tour, by the emigrant route and South Pass of the Rocky Mountains, across the continent of North America, the great desert basin, and through California, in the years 1846, 1847 ... New York: D. Appleton & company, 1975.

Powers, Stephen; with an introduction and notes, Robert F. Heizer. Tribes of California. Contributions to North American ethnologyVol. 3. Berkeley: University of California Press, 1976.

Drawn from life: California Indians in pen and brush.[compiled] by Theodora Kroeber, Albert B. Elsasser, Robert F. Heizer. Socorro, N.M.: Ballena Press, 1977.

Hart, James David. A companion to California. New York: Oxford University Press, 1978.

Starr, Kevin. Inventing the dream: California through the Progressive Era. New York: Oxford University Press, 1985.

Bancroft, Hubert Howe] ; with an introduction by Edmund G. Brown. History of California. Works of Hubert Howe BancroftVol. 18-24. [San Rafael: Bancroft Press, 1990].

Levy, Jo Ann. They saw the elephant: women in the California gold rush. Norman, Okla.: University of Oklahoma Press, 1992.

The Way we lived: California Indian stories, songs & reminiscences.Edited with commentary by Malcolm Margolin. Rev. 2nd ed. Berkeley, Calif.: Heyday Books, 1993.

Rawls, James J; edited by Leonard Nelson and Denise Culver Nelson ; illustrations by Walt Stewart and Phil Frank. California dreaming: more stories from Dr. History. New York: McGraw-Hill, Inc., 1995.

African Americans in California.Richard J. Orsi, editor, Shirley Ann Wilson Moore, consulting editor. California historyVol.75, no.3, Fall 1996. San Francisco: California Historical Society, 1996.

Lee, Gaylen D; foreword by Mark Q. Sutton. Walking where we lived: memoirs of a Mono Indian family. Norman: University of Oklahoma Press, 1998.

Contested Eden: California before the Gold Rush.Editors, Ramon A. Gutierrez and Richard J. Orsi ; illustrations editor, Anthony Kirk ; associate editor, Marlene Smith-Baranzini. California history sesquicentennial series1. Berkeley: University of California Press in association with the California Historical Society, 1998.

Many Californias: literature from the Golden State.Edited by Gerald Haslam. 2nd ed. Western literature series. Reno: University of Nevada Press, 1999.

Sacramento: gold rush legacy, metropolitan destiny.Edited by John F. Burns. 1st ed. Carlsbad, CA: Heritage Media Corp., 1999.

Holliday, J. S. Rush for riches: gold fever and the making of California. [Oakland, Calif.]: Oakland Museum of California, 1999.

A golden state: mining and economic development in gold rush California. Editors James J. Rawls and Richard J. Orsi ; associate editor Marlene Smith-Baranzini. California history sesquicentennial series2. Berkeley, Calif.: University of California Press, 1999.

Rooted in barbarous soil: people, culture, and community in Gold Rush California.Editors, Kevin Starr and Richard J. Orsi ; illustrations editor, Anthony

Kirk ; associate editor, Marlene Smith-Baranzini. California history sesqui-centennial series3. Berkeley: University of California Press, 2000.

Kurutz, K.D& Gary F. Kurutz. California calls you: the art of promoting the Golden State, 1870 to 1940. Sausalito, Calif.: Windgate Press, 2000.

Brands, H. W. The age of gold: the California Gold Rush and the new American dream. 1st ed. New York: Doubleday, 2002.

Twain, Mark. Roughing it. Mineola, N.Y.: Dover Publications, 2003.

Illustrations and Art

Eric Warp of American Warp Drive: Art Director, including cover, maps, and all final illustrations.

Judi Decker, Decker Design Solutions: Typography and Layout Design.

Tom and Sally Meyers, Tom Meyers Photography:
Most location photography.

Noel Neuburger: Mayor, Sheriff and mural photography.

Randy Smith: River from the air photography.

PI: Printers Ink
SAMCC: Sacramento Archive and Museum Collection Center.
CSL: California State Library.
SEP: Saturday Evening Post.
Images: Public Domain / Permission as appropriate.

Robin   W 80 To S.F.
To @ Turn onto
Jefferson Blvd   to   Kegel   to   Right Cummins
Blvd
To S.E. Entrance
(2) Green poles

Cummins

Kegel   Douglas

W   Sacramento

W   Capitol

West   80   East   To 80 W
                                        To 5
                                        Tracy